WEST INDIAN POETRY

An anthology for schools

Second edition

Kenneth Ramchand
Professor of West Indian Literature
University of the West Indies

Cecil Gray
formerly Director, Diploma in Education Programme
University of the West Indies

Longman Caribbean

Longman Group UK Limited,
Longman House, Burnt Mill, Harlow,
Essex CM20 2JE, England
and Associated Companies throughout the world.

Carlong Publishers Ltd,
43 second street,
Newport West,
P. O. Box 489,
kingston 10,
Jamaica

Longman (Trinidad) Limited,
Boundary Road,
San Juan,
Trinidad

Set in 91/2 12pt Zapf Book Light (Linotron)
Produced by Longman Group (FE) Ltd
Printed in Hong Kong

ISBN 0 582 76637 0

Contents

Introduction xiv

A Sea-Chantey
Derek Walcott
ST LUCIA
xix

PART ONE 1

This Land

In Our Land
Harold Telemaque
TRINIDAD & TOBAGO
2

Oh I Must Hurry
Raymond Barrow
BELIZE
3

Arawak Prologue
Basil McFarlane
JAMAICA
4

Discoverer
Edward Brathwaite
BARBADOS
6

Carrion Crows
A. J. Seymour
GUYANA
7

A Comfort of Crows
Dennis Scott
JAMAICA
8

Till I Collect
Martin Carter
GUYANA
9

Struggle and Endurance

Yusman Ali, Charcoal Seller
Ian McDonald
TRINIDAD & TOBAGO
10

The Washerwomen
Owen Campbell
ST VINCENT
11

The Castaways
Claude McKay
JAMAICA
12

Albert
A. L. Hendriks
JAMAICA
13

Ode to Brother Joe
Anthony McNeill
JAMAICA
14

Squatter's Rites
Dennis Scott
JAMAICA
15

Me Cyaan Believe it
Michael Smith
JAMAICA
17

Ad. for a Housing Scheme
Anthony McNeill
JAMAICA
20

University of Hunger
Martin Carter
GUYANA
21

from The Dust
Edward Brathwaite
BARBADOS
22

Homestead
Eric Roach
TRINIDAD & TOBAGO
24

Husks
Anthony McNeill
JAMAICA
26

Growing Up

Bird
Dennis Scott
JAMAICA
27

Flowers
Dennis Craig
GUYANA
28

The Pond
Mervyn Morris
JAMAICA
28

Pa
Victor Questel
TRINIDAD & TOBAGO
29

Ave Maria
Barbara Ferland
JAMAICA
30

Thinking Back on Yard Time
James Berry
JAMAICA
31

Roots
Harold Telemaque
TRINIDAD & TOBAGO
32

To My Mother
Eric Roach
TRINIDAD & TOBAGO
33

Encounters

Revelation
H. A. Vaughan
SANTO DOMINGO
35

Caribbean Journal
Cecil Gray
TRINIDAD & TOBAGO
35

Earth is Brown
Shana Yardan
GUYANA
36

The Saddhu of Couva
Derek Walcott
ST LUCIA
38

Tizzic
Edward Brathwaite
BARBADOS
40

Lines Written on a Train
Cecil Herbert
TRINIDAD & TOBAGO
41

Country
E. McG. Keane
ST VINCENT
42

Limbo Dancer at Immigration
John Agard
GUYANA
43

Men and Women

In Absence
H. A. Vaughan
SANTO DOMINGO
45

Family Pictures
Mervyn Morris
JAMAICA
46

Birthday Honours
Mervyn Morris
JAMAICA
47

Philpot Puzzled
E. A. Markham
MONTSERRAT
49

Anna
Derek Walcott
ST LUCIA
50

Notes on a September Day
Anthony McNeill
JAMAICA
52

Drought
Wayne Brown
TRINIDAD & TOBAGO
53

Being a Woman

Poem for Mothers
Cheryl Albury
BAHAMAS
54

Superwife
Cheryl Albury
BAHAMAS
55

Old I
Dionne Brand
TRINIDAD & TOBAGO
56

Old II
Dionne Brand
TRINIDAD & TOBAGO
56

Tell Me
Pamela Mordecai
JAMAICA
57

Summer and Kitsilano Beach
Judy Miles
TRINIDAD & TOBAGO
58

Lunch Hour
Judy Miles
TRINIDAD & TOBAGO
59

Crow Poem
Christine Craig
JAMAICA
60

Politics and Society

Mailboat to Hell
Patrick Rahming
BAHAMAS
61

This Is The Dark Time, My Love
Martin Carter
GUYANA
62

No Man's Land
Gloria Escoffery
JAMAICA
63

To the Unknown Non-Combatant
Mervyn Morris
JAMAICA
64

A White Man Considers the Situation
Ian McDonald
TRINIDAD & TOBAGO
65

Parades, Parades
Derek Walcott
ST LUCIA
66

O Dreams O Destinations
Edward Brathwaite
BARBADOS
67

Creators

Jaffo the Calypsonian
Ian McDonald
TRINIDAD & TOBAGO
69

Landscape Painter, Jamaica
Vivian Virtue
JAMAICA
71

Apologia
Frank Collymore
BARBADOS
72

For Harry Simmons
Derek Walcott
ST LUCIA
72

Vocation
Robert Lee
ST LUCIA
73

Mass Man
Derek Walcott
ST LUCIA
74

Dilemmas

Corners Without Answers
Roger McTair
(TRINIDAD & TOBAGO)
76

Will the Real Me Please
Stand Up?
A. L. Hendriks
JAMAICA
77

Theophilus Jones Walks
Naked Down King Street
Heather Royes
JAMAICA
79

Choice of Corpses
Kendel Hippolyte
JAMAICA
81

Portia Faces Life
Marc Matthews
GUYANA
82

Noah
Wayne Brown
TRINIDAD & TOBAGO
84

Adios, Carenage
Derek Walcott
ST LUCIA
86

Time, Folkways, Religion

Ol' Higue
Wordsworth A. McAndrew
GUYANA
89

Sister Mary and the Devil
Lorna Goodison
JAMAICA
91

Tabiz
Anson Gonzales
TRINIDAD & TOBAGO
93

Guard-ring
Dennis Scott
JAMAICA
94

Uncle Time
Dennis Scott
JAMAICA
96

So Long, Charlie Parker
Edward Brathwaite
BARBADOS
96

Don
Anthony McNeill
JAMAICA
98

The Tree
H. A. Vaughan
SANTO DOMINGO
99

There Runs a Dream
A. J. Seymour
GUYANA
100

PART TWO 101

This Land

Holy
George Campbell
JAMAICA
102

This Land
M. G. Smith
JAMAICA
103

The Village
William S. Arthur
BARBADOS
104

The Village
Karl Sealy
BARBADOS
105

To Those
Harold Telemaque
TRINIDAD & TOBAGO
106

Ancestor on the Auction Block
Vera Bell
JAMAICA
106

For Christopher Columbus
A. J. Seymour
GUYANA
108

The Age of Chains
E. McG. Keane
ST VINCENT
110

Islands
Roger McTair
TRINIDAD & TOBAGO
113

Like Music Suddenly
A. L. Hendriks
JAMAICA
114

Hex
Edward Brathwaite
BARBADOS
115

After the Storm
Derek Walcott
ST LUCIA
117

I Shall Return
Claude McKay
JAMAICA
118

Residue
Anthony McNeill
JAMAICA
119

Struggle and Endurance

The Riders
Barnabus Ramon-Fortuné
TRINIDAD & TOBAGO
120

All Men Come to the Hills
Roger Mais
JAMAICA
121

Death of a Comrade
Martin Carter
GUYANA
122

from Rain Mosaic
A. N. Forde
BARBADOS
123

An Old Woman
P. M. Sherlock
JAMAICA
125

March Trades
Eric Roach
TRINIDAD & TOBAGO
125

Growing Up

Children Coming from School
Roger Mais
JAMAICA
128

Still Life
Geoffrey Drayton
BARBADOS
129

Adam and Batto
Edward Brathwaite
BARBADOS
129

St Mary's Estate
Dionne Brand
TRINIDAD & TOBAGO
132

Encounters

Birthday Poem for Clifford Sealy
George W. Lamming
BARBADOS
134

Letter to Lamming in England
Eric Roach
TRINIDAD & TOBAGO
137

The Almond Trees
Derek Walcott
ST LUCIA
139

Colonisation in Reverse
Louise Bennett
JAMAICA
140

His Nerves Scraped White
Edward Brathwaite
BARBADOS
142

Men and Women

Since You
Dionne Brand
TRINIDAD & TOBAGO
145

Villanelle of the Year's End
A. L. Hendriks
JAMAICA
146

A Family Man
Dennis Scott
JAMAICA
147

At two o'clock . . . .
Judy Miles
TRINIDAD & TOBAGO
147

The Sea and the Hills (1951)
Cecil Herbert
TRINIDAD & TOBAGO
149

I Have Survived So Long
Mahadai Das
GUYANA
151

Horses
Dawad Philip
TRINIDAD & TOGABO
152

The Catherine Letter
Anthony McNeill
JAMAICA
155

Quadrille for Tigers
Christine Craig
JAMAICA
157

Elemental
Edward Baugh
JAMAICA
158

The Black Tree
Wayne Brown
TRINIDAD & TOBAGO
158

Black Friday 1962
Martin Carter
GUYANA
170

Sacred Flame
Grace Nichols
GUYANA
171

Politics and Society

I Write About
Orlando Wong
JAMAICA
160

The Slums
George Campbell
JAMAICA
161

from Sappho Sakyi's
Meditations
Edward Brathwaite
BARBADOS
162

Dutty Tough
Louise Bennett
JAMAICA
165

Afternoon Elegy
Basil McFarlane
JAMAICA
166

Caribbean Basin
Cecil Gray
TRINIDAD & TOBAGO
166

I watched the island
From *Tales of the Islands*:
Chapter X
Derek Walcott
ST LUCIA
167

Homecoming, Anse La Raye
Derek Walcott
ST LUCIA
168

Creators

Trane
Edward Brathwaite
BARBADOS
173

Birthday Poem 1970
John Figueroa
JAMAICA
174

This Poem
Edward Baugh
JAMAICA
174

Portrayal
Owen Campbell
ST VINCENT
175

The Hammer
David Rudder
TRINIDAD & TOBAGO
177

Road Mending
Barnabas Ramon-Fortuné
TRINIDAD & TOBAGO
179

Le Petit Paysan
Barbara Ferland
JAMAICA
180

Dilemmas

I Now Have Some
Twenty Years
Michael Foster
BARBADOS
181

The Castle
Mervyn Morris
JAMAICA
182

The Stenographer
Barbara Ferland
JAMAICA
184

Because I Have
turned my back
Frank Collymore
BARBADOS
184

Compassionate Spider
Anthony McNeill
JAMAICA
185

Suicide?
Judy Miles
TRINIDAD & TOBAGO
187

Time, Folkways, Religion

I Cannot Bear . . .
A. J. Seymour
GUYANA
188

The Word Once Spoken
Barnabas Ramon-Fortuné
TRINIDAD & TOBAGO
189

Judas
Mervyn Morris
JAMAICA
189

from Testament
M. G. Smith
JAMAICA
191

The Visit
Wayne Brown
TRINIDAD & TOBAGO
192

Letter for a Friend
Daniel Williams
ST VINCENT
193

The Season of Phantasmal Peace
Derek Walcott
ST LUCIA
195

Day's End
Frank Collymore
BARBADOS
196

Epitaph
Hugh Doston Carberry
JAMAICA
197

The Knife of Dawn
Martin Carter
GUYANA
197

PART THREE 199

Questions on the poems
in Part One 200

List of Poems by Author 234

Index of Titles 237

Acknowledgements

We are grateful to the following copyright holders for permission to reproduce poems:

The Author, John Agard for 'Limbo Dancer at Immigration' from *Limbo Dancer in Dark Glasses* pub. Greenhart, London 1983; the Author, William S. Arthur for 'The Village' from *Morning Glory* 1944; the Author, Raymond H. Barrow for 'Oh, I Must Hurry' from BIM Vol II, 1949 p 242; the Author, Edward Baugh for 'Elemental' & 'This Poem' from *Jamaica Journal*, Vol 4, No 1 (March 1970), p 32; Mrs. A. P. German on behalf of the Vera Bell Estate for 'Ancestor on the Auction Block' by Vera Bell (Mrs Vera Montgomery); the Author, Prof. Edward Kamau Brathwaite for 'Discoverer', part 'The Dust', 'O Dreams O Destinations' & 'His Nerves Scraped White' from *Rights of Passage* pubd. OUP 1967, 'Tizzic' from *Islands* pubd. OUP 1969, 'So long Charlie Parker' & 'Trane' from *Other Exiles* pubd. OUP 1975, 'Hex' from *Mother Poem* pubd. OUP 1977, 'Adam and Batto' from *Sun Poem* pubd. OUP 1982, & part 'Sapho Sakyi's Meditations' from BIM 26, 1958; the Author, Wayne Brown for 'Drought', 'Noah', 'The Black Tree' & 'The Visit' from *Breaklights* ed. Andrew Salkey; the Author, Owen M. Campbell for 'The Washerwomen' from BIM 13, Dec. 1950 & 'Portrayal' from *Caribbean Voices* 14.10.86; the Author, H. D. Carberry for 'Epitaph' from *A Treasury of Jamaican Poetry*, 1949; the Author, Martin Carter for 'Till I Collect', 'University of Hunger', 'This is the Dark Time of my Love', 'Death Must Not Find Us' & 'The Knife of Dawn' from *Poems of Resistance* pubd. Univ. Ghana/Lawrence & Wishart Ltd. 1964, & 'Black Friday 1962' from *Poems of Succession* pubd. New Beacon Books 1977; the Author, Christine Craig for 'Crow Poem' from *Quadrille* 821 & 'Quadrille for Tigers' from *Quadrille For Tigers* 1984; the Author, Prof. Dennis Craig for 'Flowers' from BIM 33, 1961; the Author, Mahadai Das for 'I Have Survived So Long' from *My Finer Steel Shall Grow* Vol 31 SAMEHDAT No 2, 1982; the Author, Geoffrey Drayton for 'Still Life' from *Caribbean Voices* 27.3.49; the Author, Gloria Escoffery for 'No Man's Land' from *Landscape in the Making* 1976; Faber & Faber Ltd for 'The Season of Phantasmal Peace' by Derek Walcott from *The Fortunate Traveller*; Farrar Straus & Giroux Inc for 'A Sea Chantey' & part 'I Watched the Island' from 'Tales of the Islands' from *Collected Poems 1948–1984* by Derek Walcott. Copyright © 1962, 1986 by Derek Walcott, part 'Anna' & part 'Harry Simmons' from *Another Life* by Derek Walcott. Copyright © 1972, 1973 by Derek

Walcott; the Author, Barbara Ferland for 'Ave Maria', 'Le Petit Paysan' &
'The Stenographer' from *Focus* ed. Edna Manley 1956; the Author, John
Figueroa for 'The Birthday Poem' from *Ignoring Hurts* 1976; the Author,
Alfred N. Forde for 'Rain Mosaic' from BIM 32, pp 267–70, 1961; Mr.
Denis Foster for 'I Have Seen some Twenty Years' by Michael Foster
from BIM 41 pp 43–4, 1965; Garland Publishing Ltd for 'Holy' & 'The
Slums' by George Campbell from *First Poems*, Garland Pubg. Inc. ©
1981. All rights reserved; the Author, Anton Gonzales for 'Tabiz' from
Collected Poems 1964–79, The New Voices, Diego Martin, 1979; the
Author, Lorna Goodison for 'Sister Mary and the Devil' from *Tamarind
Season*, pubd. Inst. of Jamaica 1980; the Author, A. L. Hendriks for
'Albert' from *Melanthika*, LWM Publications 1977, 'Will the Real Me
Please Stand Up?' from *Madonna of the Unknown Nation*, London
Workshop Press, 1974, 'Like Music Suddenly' from *These Green Islands*,
Bolium Press, p 14 1971 & 'Villanelle of the Year's End' from *Greenfield
Review*, Vol 12, No 3 1966; Hodder & Stoughton Educational Ltd for 'Ol'
Higue' by Wordsworth A. McAndrew from *Caribbean Poetry Now* ed.
Stewart Brown; the Author, E. McG. S. Keane for 'Country' from *L'oubli*,
p 12 Barbados 1950 & 'The Age of Chains' from BIM 17, p 48–9 1952; the
Author, John Robert Lee for 'Vocation' from *Vocation and Other Poems*,
UWI Extra Mural Dept; the Author, George Lamming for 'Birthday Poem
for Clifford Sealy' from BIM 14, p 132–3 1961; Mrs. Jessie Taylor for 'All
Men come to the Hills' by Roger Mais from *Treasury of Jamaican Poetry*
& 'Children Coming from School' by Roger Mais from *Caribbean Voices*;
the Author, E. A. Markham for 'Philpot Puzzled' from *The Wormwood
Review* Vol 19, No 2 p 159 1979 & *Human Rites* April 1984; the Author,
Marc Matthews for 'Portia Faces Life' from SAVACOU 3, 4 p 153–4 1970;
the Author, Ian A McDonald for 'Yusman Ali' from BIM 50 1970, 'A
White Man Considers the Situation' from *Greenfield Review* Vol 12,
No 3–4 1985 & 'Jaffo the Calypsonian' from *Selected Poems*, pubd. The
Labour Advocate, Guyana, Georgetown 1983 & BIM 22, p 21 1955; the
Author, Basil McFarlane for 'Arawak Prologue' from FOCUS 1948 ed.
Edna Manley & 'Afternoon Elegy' 'Four O'Clock' from FOCUS ed. Edna
Manley 1960; the Author, Anthony McNeill for 'Ode to Brother Jo',
'Husks', 'Notes on a September Day', 'Residue' & 'The Compassionate
Spider' from *Hello Ungid* (Baltimore, Peacewood Press, 1971), reprinted
in *Reel from "The Life-Movie"* Kingston, Savacou Publications 1975,
'Don' from *Reel from "The Life-Movie"*, The Catherine Letter/1' from
Credences at the Alter of Cloud Kingston, Inst. of Jamaica 1979 & 'Ad.
for a Housing Scheme' © Anthony McNeill; the Author, Roger McTair
for 'Corners without Answers' from VOICES 1962 p 8 & 'Islands' from
SAVACOU 7/8 p 102; the Author, Judy Miles for 'Summer and Kitsilano
Beach' from VOICES Vol 2 No 1 p 72 1969, 'Lunch Hour' from BIM No 45
p 16 1967, 'At Two O'Clock' from VOICES Vol 1, No 4 1965 & 'Suicide'
from BIM No 44 p 267 1967; the Author, Mrs. Pamela Mordecai for 'Tell
Me'; the Author, Mervyn Morris for 'The Pond', 'Family Pictures', 'To the
Unknown Combatant', 'The Castle' & 'Judas' from *The Pond* pubd. New
Beacon Books, London 1973 & 'Birthday Honours' from BIM 36 p 246,
1963; the Author, Grace Nichols for 'Sacred Flame' from *I Is a Long*

Memoried Woman pubd. Karnak House, London 1983; Oxford
University Press Ltd for 'Thinking Back on Yard Time' by James Berry
from *Chain of Days* © James Berry 1985; the Author, Dawad Philip for
'Horses' from *Invocations*, pubd. Featherstone Press, Brooklyn, New
York; Marian Questel for 'Pa' by Victor D. Questel, first pubd. in *Hard
Stares*, The New Voices 1982; the Author, Barnabas J. Ramon-Fortune
for 'The Riders', 'Road Mending', & 'The Word Once Spoken'; Mrs.
Roach for 'Homestead', 'To My Mother', 'March Traders' & 'Letter to
Lamming in England' by Eric Morton Roach; the Author, Heather Royes
for 'Theophilus Jones Walks Naked Down King Street' from *Jamaica
Woman* (HEB 1980); the Author, David Rudder for 'The Hammer'
calypso by David Rudder and Pelham Goddard, © The Copyright
Organisation of Trinidad and Tobago; Sangster's Bookstores Ltd for
'Colonisation in Reverse' by Louise Bennett from *Jamaica Labrish* &
'Dutty Tough' by Louise Bennett from *Selected Poems* & 'I Write About'
by Orlando Wong from SAVACOU No's 14/15 1979; the Author, Dennis
Scott for 'A Comfort of Crows', 'Squatter's Rights' & 'Uncle Time' from
Uncle Time, pubd. Univ. Pittsburgh Press, 'Bird' from *Young
Commonwealth Poets '65*. pubd. Heinemann 1966, 'Guard-Ring' & 'A
Family Man' from *Dreadwalk*, pubd. New Beacon Books 1982; the
Author, Karl Sealy for 'The Village' from BIM No 7 p 54 1946; the Author,
A. J. Seymour for 'Carrion Crows' & 'There Runs a Dream' from KYK-
OVER-AL Vol 6, No 19, 'For Christopher Columbus' from The *Guyana
Book*, Demerara 1948 & 'I Cannot Bear' from *More Poems* p 5 Guyana,
1940; the Author, Sir Philip Sherlock for 'An Old Woman' from *Ten
Poems*, The Miniature Poets 12 p 9 (B. G. 1953); Nerissa Smith as
Administratrix to the Estate of Michael Smith for his 'Me Cyaan Believe
It'; the Author, M. G. Smith for 'This Land' & part 'Testament'; Twayne
Publishers, A Division of T. K. Hall & Co for 'The Castaways' & 'I Shall
Return' from *The Selected Poems of Claude McKay*, © 1981; Ken
Ramchand on behalf of the Estate of Harold Telemaque for his 'In Our
Land', 'Roots' & 'To Those'; Mrs. Joy Vaughan Brown for 'Revelation', 'In
Absence' & 'The Tree' by Hilton A. Vaughan; the Author, Vivian Virtue
for 'Landscape Painters'; Jonathan Cape Ltd on behalf of the Author,
Derek Walcott for 'The Saddhu of Couva', 'Adios Carenage' & 'After the
Storm' from *The Star Apple Kingdom*, 'Parades, Parades' from *Sea
Grapes*, 'Homecoming: Anse La Raye' from *The Gulf* & 'The Almond
Trees' from *The Castaway* the Author, Shana Yardan for 'Earth is
Brown'.

We have unfortunately been unable to trace the copyright owners of
'Poems for Mothers' & 'Superwife' by Cheryl Albury, 'Old I', 'Old II', 'St.
Mary's Estate' & 'Since You' by Dionne Brand, 'Apologia', 'Because I
have turned my Back' & 'Day's End' by Frank Collymore, 'Lines Written
on a Train' & 'From the Sea and the Hills' by Cecil Herbert, 'Choice of
Corpses' by Kendel Hippolyte, 'Mailboat to Hell' by Patrick Rahming,
'Letter for a Friend' by Daniel Williams and would appreciate any
information which would enable us to do so.

Introduction

We sometimes come across a person calling himself the ordinary reader who says that it is sufficient to read for enjoyment, and who thinks it takes away from the pleasure if there is a requirement to study poems or to say about them anything more than 'I like this' or 'This is good'. In addition, there are adults who claim that they do not care for poetry because they were forced to study it in school. Others insist that their interest in poetry has come about in spite of their experience of it at school.

The poems of this collection have been chosen to appeal to readers who wish to be able to enjoy West Indian poetry from its beginnings to the most recent times. But the arrangement according to themes and the inclusion of discussion guidelines make it obvious that it is mainly for young people preparing for an examination. To that end all the poems set for the CXC examination have been included.

The approach to poetry that you have been or are being exposed to could turn you against it or help you to enjoy it more. A lot depends on the teachers' attitudes, insight, and teaching skills, as well as on the selection of poems used. Well-selected poems provide a basis of interest that sustains careful study, with the discipline and perseverance to extract a deeper quota of enjoyment. They encourage you to make the effort, to work at a poem, to draw out as much of its juice as you can.

For that is what happens when we study a poem in a systematic and analytical way. We do not murder and dissect it as superficial readers often suggest. Rather we give birth to it in our minds and we embrace it to let

it touch our feelings. The more energy we spend looking
for the elements that went into the creation of the
poem, understanding the choices the poet made and
why, the more we grow to appreciate and respect the
powers of a creative imagination, and the more our
intellectual pleasure and enjoyment deepens and
widens. The more we discover of the elements that
went into the making of the poem, the more we respect
the way the creative imagination can transform what is
ordinary and familiar.

To illustrate that let us briefly consider the sonnet by
John Keats named 'On First Looking Into Chapman's
Homer'. Two hundred years before Keats wrote that
sonnet Chapman had translated a Greek epic poem by
Homer who lived more than two thousand years before.
The person in the sonnet tells us that when he read the
translation by Chapman he felt:

> . . . like some watcher of the skies
> When a new planet swims into his ken;
> Or like stout Cortez, when with eagle eyes
> He stared at the Pacific — and all his men
> Look'd at each other with a wild surmise —
> Silent, upon a peak in Darien.

If you knew that Keats had read that the astronomer
William Herschel had discovered the planet Uranus in
1781, long before the sonnet was written, you might
think he was referring to Herschel as 'some watcher of
the skies' though there is no proof of that. Be that as it
may, you would realise that the sonnet is neither a
celebration of Herschel's achievement nor a record of
the startling discovery of an ocean. What a reader
responds to in the sonnet are Keats' similes, linking the
experience of reading a great piece of literature with the
experience of seeing a startling new world or coming
upon an unexpected immensity of ocean. It does not
give you a report to be checked on by reading about
Herschel; nor are we tempted to take marks away from
Keats for getting his facts wrong, and attributing to
Cortez Balboa's 'discovery' of the Pacific.

Thus we take care to recognise the real content of a

poem, just as we need to take care to observe the way it is written, i.e. its forms and style. Now, despite what might be done in schools in preparation for examinations, studying the way a poem is written does not mean merely picking out the things like similes and allusions, breaking up the poem into dry crumbs. That pointless labelling of elements of the form and style of the poem misses the target and cheats you of the chance to experience the whole essence of the poem. The point of studying the poem's elements of form and style is to ensure that the organic wholeness of the poem impinges itself on your consciousness. It is done as the means of identifying and receiving the experience.

In other words if we do not bother to consider the significance of the poet's choice and placing of phrases, words, comparison, metre, and so on, we are likely to miss completely what we should experience in reading the poem, unless the poem is not a very good one. Giving the style of a poem that careful consideration, then, adds a great deal to our enjoyment as it leads us to see how our experience of the poem is directly related to the deliberate choices the poet made in putting it together.

Useful Knowledge and Information

To study a poem completely we sometimes need to apply or use different kinds of knowledge, and draw upon information from a wide range of sources. But it must be remembered that the information is a means to an end and not an end in itself. If you use information to help you to understand the poem better you are placing information in its right perspective. Quite often, however, readers make the mistake of thinking that having a lot of information about a poem is the same as experiencing or enjoying the poem. Here is an incomplete list of different kinds of material we could draw upon in our study of poems:

1 The type or genre into which the poem seems to fit
2 The social, cultural, and intellectual conditions where and when the poem was written

3 Information on the life of the author and of persons in his/her circle

4 Other poems and works by the same author

5 Poems and works by other authors of his/her time

Knowledge of such matters could enhance an understanding of the poet's thoughts and feelings so that the reader enters more fully into the world of the poem. Wherever possible the reader should garner such help towards a more insightful reading of the work. Other areas that are sometimes helpful include:

6 The way the language was spoken and written at the time the poem was composed

7 The accepted practices in literature and art at the time

8 Any other trend in literature at the time

9 The way the poem fits into the history of poetry of that country

10 Whether the printed poem is exactly the same as the original written by the author

11 What has been said by critics and other commentators about the poem and about other works by the same author

Critics and Other Commentators

Of course few poems require to be read with all those things in mind all at once, and most of those things can only be found out by more mature readers and literary scholars. And among literary scholars there are those who specialise in just one area or another. For example, scholars who concentrate on the authors' texts have little time to produce literary biographies; while many literary scholars are not really in the business of cultivating sensitivity or responsiveness to texts. It is the literary critic as reader of texts who uses the background material supplied by literary scholars to point readers to a better appreciation of the poet's work.

Yet even among those who are called literary critics there is some confusion as to what they are doing. Some use literary texts to talk about culture and society. Some are more interested in social studies. Some are really engaged in the sociology of literature, and so on. The crucial point is that for some literary critics the poem is evidence or illustration of another subject, and a dull poem or story which refers directly to what the critic is interested in is regarded as more valuable than one that has greater literary merit. Others, on the other hand, pay close attention to words and their arrangements, regarding literary texts as highly evocative and personal communications of sentiments and ideas, messages from the deepest, most obscure levels of consciousness.

Those divergent interests are now affecting the teaching of literature in schools. The practice of regarding the content of a poem or novel merely as an example of a viewpoint on a theme or topic has taken hold. It is easier to teach a theme like 'the individual in a small society' referring selectively to a group of novels and poems than to teach each novel and each poem as itself first. And it is less troublesome to concentrate on comprehension than to encourage students to respond to the ambiguities in a text. Poetry has a great deal to say about the individual, society and the world. It deals in emotions as well as ideas. It contributes to our emotional and spiritual development. But it does so best if we begin by placing the emphasis on making ourselves better readers of texts.

But that is not to say you always have to read everything with the same intensity. You will certainly find that the kind of reading you do at a given time will depend on your purpose or purposes at the time, as well as on the kind of text in your hand. Some texts, like mass circulation romances and action novels, are for casual surface reading to kill time or to escape into fantasy. We do not, therefore, apply the same criteria to all kinds of reading and all kinds of texts. We might say that a good book is one that is capable of being read at different levels. And a good reader may be defined as one who is capable of reading at different levels by choice. Such a reader does not ask Mills and Boon to be Tolstoy, and would not attempt to look at Shakespeare with the same reduced attention to words that he or she would give to reading Mandrake the Magician. That adaptability which all good readers have is what teachers seek to develop in all their students. But how does one become a good reader?

Becoming a Better Reader

It is sometimes said that the more one reads the better one becomes at it, and that is all you have to do to become a good reader. But a person who only reads comic books becomes a better reader of comics, not a better reader at different levels. That requires exposure to a wide range of reading material as well as some sort of training to help the reader with set habits to overcome problems he/she meets with in the techniques and approaches of different authors.

Focusing our attention on poetry, we can say that the study of poetry is, to the reading of poetry, what expert coaching is to sport. Class discussions along the right lines help students to venture their responses to the ideas and emotions in a poem, and to learn to recognise the part that the intelligent and imaginative use of language plays in conveying those emotions and ideas. Every such discussion should not only illumine the poem being discussed but help to build up our reading power so that we become better readers of poetry in general. The end purpose of it all is to enable each student to understand and enjoy poems independently, and to carry this ability with him beyond the school situation.

A Sea-Chantey

Là, tout n'est qu'ordre et beauté,
Luxe, calme, et volupté.

Anguilla, Adina,
Antigua, Cannelles,
Andreuille, all the l's,
Voyelles, of the liquid Antilles,

5   The names tremble like needles
Of anchored frigates,
Yachts tranquil as lilies,
In ports of calm coral,
The lithe, ebony hulls

10 Of strait-stitching schooners,
The needles of their masts
That thread archipelagoes
Refracted embroidery
In feverish waters

15 Of the sea-farer's islands,
Their shorn, leaning palms,
Shaft of Odysseus,
Cyclopic volcanoes,
Creak their own histories,

20 In the peace of green anchorage;
Flight, and Phyllis,
Returned from the Grenadines,
Names entered this sabbath,
In the port-clerk's register;

25 Their baptismal names,
The sea's liquid letters,
Repos donnez a cils...
And their blazing cargoes
Of charcoal and oranges;

30 Quiet, the fury of their ropes.
Daybreak is breaking
On the green chrome water,
The white herons of yachts
Are at sabbath communion,

35 The histories of schooners
Are murmured in coral,
Their cargoes of sponges
On sandspits of islets
Barques white as white salt

40 Of acrid Saint Maarten,
Hulls crusted with barnacles,
Holds foul with great turtles,
Whose ship-boys have seen
The blue heave of Leviathan,

45 A sea-faring, Christian,
And intrepid people.

Now an apprentice washes his cheeks
With salt water and sunlight.

In the middle of the harbour
50 A fish breaks the Sabbath
With a silvery leap.
The scales fall from him
In a tinkle of church-bells;
The town streets are orange
55 With the week-ripened sunlight,
Balanced on the bowsprit
A young sailor is playing
His grandfather's chantey
On a trembling mouth-organ.
60 The music curls, dwindling
Like smoke from blue galleys,
To dissolve near the mountains.
The music uncurls with
The soft vowels of inlets.
65 The christening of vessels,
The titles of portages,
The colours of sea-grapes,
The tartness of sea-almonds,
The alphabet of church-bells,
70 The peace of white horses
The pastures of ports,
The litany of islands,
The rosary of archipelagoes,
Anguilla, Antigua,
75 Virgin of Guadeloupe,
And stone-white Grenada
Of sunlight and pigeons,
The amen of calm waters,
The amen of calm waters,
80 The amen of calm waters.

Derek Walcott

How to Study a Poem
There can be no formula for studying a poem, but it is
possible to compile a list of steps to be followed in

nearly all cases. Though some flexibility will always be called for, it is possible to suggest a sequence in which these should be performed.

(a) Silent Readings

The poem should be read through silently, at least twice. One of the main purposes at this stage is to take the poem as a whole, so it is better not to stop at any point to puzzle out difficult or unclear sections. This reading introduces the subject matter of the poem. In Derek Walcott's 'A Sea-Chantey', for instance, we pick up 'islands', 'ships', 'the sea', 'inter-island shipping', a Sunday morning, a small town by a harbour, church bells, the sound of a mouth-organ, and smoke rising up in the hills in the still air. Although this is a silent reading, we cannot miss the reverential tone of the opening lines

> Anguilla, Adina,
> Antigua, Cannelles,
> Andreuille, all the l's,
> Voyelles, of the liquid Antilles,
> The names tremble like needles

nor can we fail to register the prayer-like quality at the close. We do not stop to analyse, but we respond to the colours like white, green, orange, and to a sense of rest after furious activity. In other words we pick up a sense of the feel of the poem, its tone and mood, without being able as yet to make a definite statement as to what the poem is about. This initial contact with the poem is crucial, since it is the first impression, the one that can incline us to become better acquainted or suggest to us what to look out for in subsequent readings.

A poem is a series of markings on a flat surface (usually print on a page), and an arrangement of sounds in space. That is, the poem is a physical entity existing for the eye as well as the ear. So *in the next two stages we might decide to concentrate on the physical properties of the poem, beginning with what we can see.*

(b) Examining Visual Properties

The decision that it is a poem before us and not a piece of prose was based on visual evidence that most readers register without thinking; we have the arrangement into lines, and variation in the lengths of lines. We also notice the space between groups of lines, that is, the arrangement into stanzas or verse paragraphs or sections. In some poems, every line begins with a capital letter and this is another kind of visual evidence that is sometimes available.

But there is a lot more to see before we get down to reading the poem. In the case of Walcott's poem there is a title 'A Sea-Chantey'; and two lines in French which rhyme, and which we assume come from a French poem. (This is called an epigraph.) We now have to think about the title. Titles usually provide a clue as to what we can expect, and since a great deal of the pleasure in reading poems comes from the creation of expectations followed by fulfilment, lack of fulfilment, or surprising fulfilment, it is worth exploring the title. The word sounds like 'chant', can suggest 'song or rhythmic utterance' and resembles the Hindi 'shantih' which is a blessing or benediction. We have to work, however, not only with connotation or suggestion, but with literal meaning, what the word denotes according to the dictionary. So we find out that a chanty (chantey) is a song sung by sailors in rhythm with their work. Walcott calls his poem 'A Sea-Chantey' not to be tautological, but to suggest, perhaps, a chanty sung by people or even by the sea itself as it does its work. Walcott the literary artist is producing a literary version of a kind of folk song called a chantey, in the same way that Wordsworth and Coleridge wrote literary ballads imitating and adapting the ballads of tradition.

Our expectations are added to by the epigraph. It is of some interest to know that the lines come from a poem by Baudelaire, though the main thing is to translate them: 'There, it is all order and beauty/Splendour stillness and delight.' The epigraph makes us wonder whether Walcott is going to produce a kind of work-song as the title implies, or whether he is going to take the same exotic view of the islands as the European poet does.

We can notice right away that the lines in Walcott's poem are short, ranging between six and nine syllables, and that there are not many rhymes at the end of the lines (end-rhymes). There are, however, 47 lines where there is an 's' at the end; and we see that lines 78, 79 and 80 are identical ('The amen of calm waters.'). These features picked up by the eye will be reinforced when we consider the poem as an object existing for the ear as well.

As we continue to look at the physical features of the poem, we note that there are no stanzas (groups of lines forming a pattern, usually indicated by a rhyme scheme). But the space between lines 46 and 47, and between lines 48 and 49 divide the poem into three sections, comprising lines 1–46, lines 47–48 and lines 49–80 respectively.

From the visual evidence then, we conclude that the poem has three sections or movements, and the visual prominence as well as the numerical peculiarity of the second section suggest to us that it will be necessary to account for lines 47 and 48 in some special way.

All this sizing up of the poem should have the effect of making us anxious to get down to reading it again. *But this time we should read it aloud, trying to come to terms with it as an arrangement of sounds.* This is not easy. Few readers can read a poem aloud the first time they see it, without stumbling in places or putting the wrong emphasis in others. So first, the poem should be read, letting the mouth shape the words, but only letting the sound be heard in the head. After this it may be read aloud two or three times either to oneself or in class. (The value of having students read out lines of a poem in class, two or three of them reading the same lines, cannot be over-estimated.)

Preliminary Technical Notes
The smallest unit in the poem as something to be heard is the syllable. Some syllables are uttered with more *loudness*, take up more *time* (*duration*), and have a

higher *pitch* than others. For convenience we say that
such syllables have more stress, and again purely for
convenience, we divide syllables into stressed or strong
and unstressed or weak. To show a stressed syllable
most books use an acute accent over the stressed
syllable and to indicate that a syllable is less stressed or
unstressed a small 'ă' is inserted above. A line is an
arrangement not of words but of stressed and relatively
unstressed syallabus thus: The námes trémble like néedles.

Syllables may fall into certain recognisable
combinations involving one stressed syllable plus either
one or two unstressed syllables. These combinations are
called feet, and the main traditional feet have names.
Those that begin with the unstressed syllable are said to
be *rising*:

> the iamb: cŏmpóse; ăt leást,
> the anapest: ăt ă glánce; ăftĕrnóon

Those that begin with the stressed syllable are said to
be *falling*:

> the trochee: jínglĕ, eńdĕd
> the dactyl: eḿphăsĭs, ańchŏrăgĕ

Traditional feet, especially the iamb, which is the
commonest foot in English, are still used by modern
poets. It should be noted that while educated West
Indians can recognise feet in English English poetry or
American English poetry, our pronunciation is not
exactly like theirs and we may be hearing them a little
differently. (In our writing we may be in danger of using
two systems of accentuation or more, unknowingly, as
some of our early poets tended to do.) But there is a
freer system of scansion wherein the number of
unstressed syllables is more variable and is not limited
to two. In this system, we hardly need the term 'foot'; all
we need to do is to recognise the recurrence of the
strong stress. Some critics advocate this method of
scansion for all poetry in English. Its only disadvantage
is that, without the marks over the unstressed syllables,
the beginning student might find it harder to recognise
when there is deliberate resort to traditional feet.

Poems that make use of these traditional feet to produce a recognisable pattern in the line (this includes the number of syllables and the number of feet) are said to have metre. Poems that do not observe regularity in these respects are said to be in free verse. We can retain these terms only if we remember that metre here means regular and fairly recognisable metre, but we should be prepared to find that free verse is regulated in its own way i.e., it has its own metre.

Hearing 'A Sea-Chantey'
The vowels and consonants in the opening lines of 'A Sea-Chantey' strike us at once.

> Anguilla, Adina
> Antigua, Canelles
> Andreuille, all the l's
> Voyelles, of the liquid Antilles

The long vowels and diphthongs lengthen out the line and can suggest languor or slow relish. The liquid l's and sibilant s's suggest the sound of the sea and the flow of water. Alliteration (repetitions of the consonants 'l' and 's') and assonance (repetition of vowel sounds) contribute to our sense of a chant or prayer. The opening lines, in other words, help to establish, by their sound, the languorous mood of the poem, they convey an attitude of awe or invocation, and they make us aware of the sensuous presence of the sea.

There are other kinds of sound effects at work on the first hearing. In the shortened lines 45–46 which come at the end of the first section of the poem, we find that the stresses (called strong stresses) have been made to occur quite close to one another, giving emphasis to the poet's summation of the qualities of the people who live in the islands he is writing about: 'A séa-fáring Chrístian/And intrépid péople'. Lines 47–48 which follow stand out partly because they are longer lines and partly because the rhythm changes, becoming more like the rhythms of normal speech: 'Now an apprentice washes his cheeks/With salt water and sunlight'. These lines lead into the almost prosy movement of lines

49–62 in which the poet appears to be recording ordinary Sunday morning sights and sounds.

A poet can vary the verse rhythm (i.e. the metre, which is only part of the total rhythm of a poem) of his poem. When we hear the poem, we pick these variations up intuitively. The combination of rhythmic effects in lines 69–80 (repetition of words, grammatical structures and stress patterns) is made more emphatic by the fact that most of the lines are end-stopped (they have a full pause). Lines 63–68 illustrate the point. The effect of all this is to make the poem sound like a litany and this comes to a climax in lines 78–80 which consist of 'The amen of calm waters' repeated three times like a benediction.

It would be dishonest to pretend that after our silent reading, and after our visual inspection of the poem we have not picked up any of the meanings of the poem. In fact, our response to the sounds is to some extent guided by that rough understanding. For pure sound can be associated with a wide range of meanings and it is only by admitting the meanings of the words that we can discover the appropriateness and effectiveness of the sounds.

The more we understand the poem, the more we will hear. But on a first or second hearing aloud certain features emerge. The three-part division that we were able to see on visual inspection is matched by three different patterns of orchestration of sound. Section one begins with awe and languorousness, and builds up to a plain declaration of the qualities and character of the islanders. Section two focuses, in a matter-of-fact way, upon an action which, as we shall see, is an act of initiation, an induction into the life of the sea and the traditions of island life. Section three builds up as we have seen, to a religious climax (a climax to the whole system of religious reference and religious imagery running through the poem) with the benediction 'The amen of calm waters/The amen of calm waters/The amen of calm waters'.

By the time we have completed the first three stages – namely, silent reading, visual scrutiny and reading aloud, we will have experienced the poem. That is, we will have felt the emotions the poem wants to evoke and we will have done so, whether we know it or not, because of the poet's arrangement of sounds and his word choices which include his use of figurative language such as metaphors, similes and other stylistic devices.

So we are now ready to move in closer to the poem to make sure that we can do two things: (i) we should try and understand enough to be able to offer a rough paraphrase; and (ii) we should make ourselves able to provide a general description of the kind of poem we are dealing with.

At this stage therefore we mark or underline words and phrases we don't understand, using dictionaries and reference books to work out meanings. Although a good poem cannot be paraphrased satisfactorily, it is essential that we are able to put in our own words the literal meaning of the poem. When we have done the best paraphrase we can, we should attempt to formulate a summary. The purpose of the summary is to force us to decide what is for us the most important idea or feeling of the poem.

With a paraphrase and summary behind us we can attempt to answer two very basic questions. The first relates to the person we imagine speaking the poem. We have to tell ourselves early on whether the person speaking is a character in the poem or somebody standing outside the poem. If he is standing outside the poem, is he speaking directly about his emotions (as the poet or an aspect or persona of the poet), or is he speaking authoritatively as somebody who knows past, present, and even future about the subject matter? In 'A Sea-Chantey' the speaker is not a character in the poem, and the voice is not speaking directly about its own personal emotions; it is the voice of someone who knows the islands, the islanders and their history.

Once we get some kind of focus on the person speaking we are in a position to talk about his attitude to the subject matter, to the reader, and to himself. These three attitudes make up the *tone* of the poem.

The speaker's attitude to the subject matter is the most significant part of the tone of 'A Sea-Chantey' for, as we shall see, the poem is really a celebration of the life of islands and islanders.

From here, there is nothing for it but to move through the poem section by section or stanza by stanza, allowing ourselves to respond as fully as possible as we go along. But after all this it can happen that students are at a loss when asked to write about a poem. In a discussion many ideas are thrown up. And as a poem is followed line by line, many reactions are made. It is not well enough recognised that the inability to write about a poem more often comes from having too much to say than too little. How does one put it all together in the form of an essay or appreciation?

The answer is that one doesn't put it all together. *An essay on a poem is an essay on selected aspects of the poem*; an apppreciation of a poem is an account of what one considers the most important and interesting things about a poem. In studying a poem we work at making as full a response as possible to everything that is present. Writing about a poem obliges us to select and arrange. Where a specific question is posed, like 'Write on animal imagery in the poem printed below' the student has the selection made for him; but when the question says 'Write an appreciation of the poem printed below' the student is being called upon to make the selection himself. A trained and sensitive reader very often fixes at once upon what is most important. But even such a reader would do well to study the poem systematically, survey it as it were, if only to make sure that because of his own preferences and biases he doesn't neglect important areas in the work. This is where the notion of *theme* comes into play.

We can say by way of convenient definition that the theme of a literary work is what the work is really about. Our sense of this emerges from our recognition of what the subject matter of the poem is, and from our picking up from the preliminary readings what is the attitude of the poem or poet to the subject matter. It can bear repetition. The theme of a poem is not the same as the subject matter of the poem. The subject matter of Walcott's 'A Sea-Chantey' is a group of islands and the life of the islanders from generation to generation. But what is its theme?

Most commentators on Walcott's poetry are silent or vague on this score. A number of teachers avoid it in the CXC class because they are unable to find a theme or find much depth in the one handed out to them. It is obvious from the reverential opening, and from the benediction at the close, that Walcott's poem is some kind of celebration of the islands and of the life of the islanders. But the poem makes no concession to those who want poems to speak directly on a subject of great relevance. It is, therefore, a good extreme case to use to make the point that a poem makes its essential communication subliminally, indirectly, and mainly through the senses and not primarily, though the age demands it, as thought or prose argument to be extracted by rapid reading or memorised from what critics say.

'A Sea-Chantey' is a highly nationalistic poem. It repudiates the notion contained in the epigraph from Baudelaire that the islands are exotic by showing a life of toil and unspectacular heroism. And it denies the assertion of so many, since the British historian James Anthony Froude first declared it, that there are no people here. The poem offers a picture of a people facing hurricanes, volcanic eruptions, storms at sea and strange creatures of the deep as they ply the routes between islands extracting a living from the watery element.

The islanders, the poem emphatically declares in lines 45 and 46, are 'A sea-faring, Christian,/And intrepid people.' They have been engaging with the sea for generations, trading in sponges, in salt, in fruit and vegetables. There is a tradition. So a young sailor plays his grandfather's chantey; and on a bright sabbath morning a young man dedicates himself, sacramentally, to the life on the sea: 'Now an apprentice washes his cheeks/With salt water and sunlight.'

As colonials, the islanders have had the history and

culture of the coloniser thrust upon them so they either have no history or are copiers of other people's history.

Walcott uses the unusual syntax of the first 19 lines to deny historylessness and to assert not only that we have a history but also our own sense of what constitutes glory. We move through the nouns and noun phrases of the first 18 lines panting for the verb, until in line 19 we get 'creak their own histories'. This doesn't make life at all easy for us. For now we have to decide which of the noun groups is the subject of the verb. Until we realise that the whole 'catalogue of alliterative names, scenic vistas, sounds and conceits,' everything indeed that pertains to the islands and islanders, all of them speak of the life and soul of the place, all of them creak their own authentic history.

The first 46 lines of 'A Sea-Chantey' say a lot if we literally listen to them, pick up the tone and the poet's attitude, and groping towards a discovery of the theme, respond to the figurative language employed.

Two main sets of imagery are introduced in this part of the poem. There is first of all what some critics call the conceit.

The ships moving between the islands are like thread moving through the eyes of needles; the schooners stitch the straits; the masts are needles; the foam in the wake of the ships is like embroidery.

The first function of these images drawn from sewing and embroidery is to suggest the way in which inter-island trading knits the islands together as one.

The second function is to add to the portrait of the life of the islanders. The imagery drawn from sewing, needlework and embroidery suggests that the poet wants to include those who stay at home but who are equally heroic.

With the introduction of the 'lithe ebony hills' of the schooners in line 9 (the 'lithe' and 'ebony' suggest the people), we begin to construct the hard journeys of the islanders from the decks of whose vessels shorn coconut trees and gouged-out craters can be seen, portents of calamity to those in passing ships.

Without narrative and without direct statement, the

poet tells between lines 9 and 19 about the arduous toil
of a sea-faring people who have a religious attitude,
people who face the sea and the forces of nature and
maintain a sense of awe and circumspect behaviour.

Walcott has no problem calling his islanders
Christians because that is a fact of their situation and
because his interest is in the religious attitude and in
the existence of custom, ritual and ceremony.

The poem begins with an invocation and ends with
a benediction. Between lines 20 and 30 a cessation of
activity is evoked as the ships come into harbour and
their ropes hang slack, but 'In the peace of green
anchorage', their 'blazing cargoes of charcoal and
oranges' take on the shape of an offering on the altar.

The system of religious reference and religious
imagery enforces the patriotic and celebratory quality of
the poem.

A young man, presumably on a boat, washes his face
in the sea. The poem says, 'Now an apprentice washes
his cheeks/With salt water and sunlight.' The word
'apprentice' suggests that he is in training for the life on
the sea or the life in the islands. Intuitively, we
recognise that there is a kind of baptism being
described, an immersion in place and the life of the
place, an induction or initiation. The young man
washes his cheeks with sunlight and salt water
accepting the heavenly light and the necessity for sweat
and toil on the sea.

From this highly ritualistic moment, the poem turns
in line 49 to an evocation of scenes in the small harbour
town on a sabbath morning. But now every movement,
every sound is charged with symbolic meaning. A fish
leaps out of the water, the church bell is ringing, the
quiet streets are bathed in sunlight and on a boat
somewhere a young sailor is playing on his mouth-
organ a chantey learnt from his grandfather (another of
the poem's ways of suggesting a tradition almost in
defiance of the view that these islands have no history
to be proud of).

Again, these apparently disconnected events are
made to connect with one another. Everything is sacred,

every act an act of worship. The music of the mouth-organ rises like smoke from the boats' galleys up to the mountains. This is literal enough.

But from this music (60–62), the poem moves boldly to the music of people and place; lines 64–71 point reverentially to familiar details and by line 72 we have moved out of the one harbour back to the chain of islands seen as 'litany of islands' and 'rosary of archipelagos', back indeed to the islands named at the start which are now given final benediction.

Kenneth Ramchand

PART ONE

This Land

In Our Land

In our land,
Poppies do not spring
From atoms of young blood,
So gaudily where men have died:
5   In our land
Stiletto cane blades
Sink into our hearts,
And drink our blood.

In our land,
10 Sin is not deep,
And bends before the truth,
Asking repentantly for pardon:
In our land
The ugly stain
15 That blotted Eden garden
Is sunk deep only.

In our land
Storms do not strike
For territory's fences,
20 Elbow room, nor breathing spaces:
In our land
The hurricane
Of clashes break our ranks
For tint of eye.

25 In our land
    We do not breed
    That taloned king, the eagle,
    Nor make emblazonry of lions;
    In our land,
30 The black birds
    And the chickens of our mountains
    Speak our dreams.

Harold Telemaque
b. TOBAGO 1909

Oh I Must Hurry

Oh I must hurry, I must hurry out
To the unspoiled savannahs of El Cayo,
Where the flat grass rolls out into the haze
And the primenta flare their fans
5 In protest of the sun's insistence.

Oh I must lay my heart, lay my soul
Deep in the hidden silence of the ridge
Where the thick pines spire their rugged beauty
With a wanton's disregard for being.

10 Stamp on my eye's retina
    The glory of the Mayan hills
    Silent and gaunt with knowledge of a time
    Of pagan sacrifice and ancient lore.
    To these
15 The mossy terrace of Xunán Tunich
    Still look askance with mute allegiance;
    Though the tall stand of sapodilla trees,
    Tearing through chiseled stelae,
    Voices derisive mockery of dead Mayan power.

20 Shudder the hills in the misty mornings
Up where the steep mule-trails
Contort through bushy tunnels;
Shudder the hills till the sun
Lights up with equatorial lordliness
25 And the wild deer stretch themselves
And traipse to where the cool creek-water spews
Along the marl-clay banks of twisting rivers.

Cry from the tall mahogany
The gay-plumed macaw; and high overhead
30 The chatter of green parakeets
Winging for morning feed.
Rain on the pine-ridge: rain steadily pouring,
Like God capsizing from His open palm
Handfuls of rain-dust, silver and black and grey.
35 Or a slow misty drizzle; here and there
He shakes a laundry-man's sprinkle
In scattered patterns on the dry brown foliage.

Oh I must hurry, I must hurry out
And photograph the imagery
40   of these upon my mind,
Lest To-morrow erect its impossible wall
With yet another of my ultimate regrets.

Raymond Barrow
b. BELIZE 1920

Arawak Prologue

We cross many rivers, but here is no anguish; our
dugouts have straddled the salt sea. The land
we have found is a mountain, magical with birds'
throats, and in the sea are fish. In the forests are many
5 fleet canoes. And here is no anguish, though storms
still the birds and frighten the fish from inshore shallows. And
once it seemed the mountain moved, groaning
a little.

In the sunless wet, after
rains, leaves in the tangled underbrush (like cool hands
of children on face and arms) glisten. I
am not one for society, and think how the houses throb with the noise
of women up to their elbows
in cassava milk, when the dove-grey sea's breast is
soft in the lowering light – and the land we found
fairest of women.

That bright day, the light
like clusters of gold fruit, alone, unknown
of any, the dugout and I fled the shore's
burning beauty; the first wave's shock
an ecstasy like singing, oh, and the sea's strength
entered these arms. All day
we climbed the hill
of the sea.

It seemed I died
and found that bleak
Coyaba of the wise. The dugout
faltered in a long smooth swell. There were houses on the
water, aglow with light and music and strange
laughter. Like great birds, with
ominous mutterings and preenings, they
hovered on every side. Flat on the dugout's
bottom, I prayed deliverance. Where was the land, the
houses throbbing with the noise of women
up to their elbows in cassava milk?
                                        The towering birds
floated majestically on, dragging me a little in their
fabulous wake.

                    I tell this story in the evening, after
the smoke of pipes has addled the elders'
brains, and I am assured at least of the children's respectful
silence. I am no longer certain it happened to me.

Basil McFarlane
b. JAMAICA 1922

Discoverer

Columbus from his after-
deck watched stars, absorbed in water,
melt in liquid amber drifting

through my summer air.
5 Now with morning, shadows lifting,
beaches stretched before him cold and clear.

Birds circled flapping flag and mizzen
mast: birds harshly hawking, without fear.
Discovery he sailed for was so near.

10 Columbus from his after-
deck watched heights he hoped for,
rocks he dreamed, rise solid from my simple water.

Parrots screamed. Soon he would touch
our land, his charted mind's desire.
15 The blue sky blessed the morning with its fire.

But did his vision
fashion, as he watched the shore,
the slaughter that his soldiers

furthered here? Pike
20 point and musket butt,
hot splintered courage, bones

cracked with bullet shot,
tipped black boot in my belly, the
whip's uncurled desire?

25 Columbus from his after-
deck saw bearded fig trees, yellow pouis
blazed like pollen and thin

waterfalls suspended in the green
as his eyes climbed towards the highest ridges
30 where our farms were hidden.

Now he was sure
he heard soft voices mocking in the leaves.
What did this journey mean, this
new world mean: dis-
35 covery? Or a return to terrors
he had sailed from, known before?

I watched him pause.

Then he was splashing silence.
Crabs snapped their claws
40 and scattered as he walked towards our shore.

Edward Brathwaite
b. BARBADOS 1930

Carrion Crows

Yes, I have seen them perched on paling posts –
Brooding with evil eyes upon the road,
Their black wings hooded – and they left these roosts

When I have hissed at them. Away they strode
5 Clapping their wings in a man's stride, away
Over the fields. And I have seen them feast
On swollen carrion in the broad eye of day,
Pestered by flies, and yet they never ceased.

But I have seen them emperors of the sky,
10 Balancing gracefully in the wind's drive
With their broad sails just shifting, or again
Throwing huge shadows from the sun's eye
To brush so swiftly over the field's plain,
And winnowing the air like beauty come alive.

A. J. Seymour
b. GUYANA 1914

A Comfort of Crows

Mark this for a mercy: that here
birds, even here, sustain
the wide and impossible highways
of warm currents, divide the sky;
5   mark this – they all day have
amazed the air, that it falls apart
from their heavy wings in thin wedges
of sound; though the dull black earth
is very still, sweating
10   a special sourness
they make high over the hard thorn-trees
their own magnificence, turning,
they chain all together
with very slow journeys to and fro
15   the limits of the dead place,
smelling anything old and no longer quick.

Even here, though the rough ground
offers no kindness to the eye
nor the rusting engines could not ever
20   have intended an excellence of motion
and the stones have fallen in strange attitudes
and the boxes full of dry stained paper—
above the harsh barrows of land and metal
great birds pursue a vigilant silence.
25   The ceremonies of their soaring
have made a new and difficult solace:
there is no dead place nor dying so terrible
but weaves above it surely, breaking
the fragile air with beauty of its coming,
30   a comfort as of crows...

Dennis Scott
b. JAMAICA 1939

Till I Collect

Over the shining mud the moon is blood
falling on ocean at the fence of lights.
My mast of love will sail and come to port
leaving a trail beneath the world, a track
5   cut by my rudder tempered out of anguish.

The fisherman will set his tray of hooks
and ease them one by one into the flood.
His net of twine will strain the liquid billow
and take the silver fishes from the deep.
10   But my own hand I dare not plunge too far
lest only sand and shells I bring to air
lest only bones I resurrect to light.

Over the shining mud the moon is blood
falling on ocean at the fence of lights—
15   My course I set, I give my sail the wind
to navigate the islands of the stars
till I collect my scattered skeleton
till I collect...

Martin Carter
b. GUYANA 1927

Struggle and Endurance

Yusman Ali, Charcoal Seller

Some men have lives of sweet and seamless gold.
No dent of dark or harshness mars those men.
Not Yusman Ali though, not that old charcoal man
Whose heart I think has learned to break a hundred times a day.
5 He rides his cart of embered wood in a long agony.

He grew rice and golden apples years ago
He made an ordinary living by the long mud shore,
Laughed and drank rum like any other man and planned his four sons' glory
His young eyes watched the white herons rise like flags
10 And the sun brightening on the morning water in his fields.
His life fell and broke like a brown jug on a stone.
In middle age his four sons drowned in one boat up a pleasant river,
The wife's heart cracked and Yusman Ali was alone, alone, alone.
Madness howled in his head. His green fields died.

15 He burns the wild wood in his barren yard alone,
Sells the charcoal on the villaged coast and feasts on stars at night.
Thinness makes a thousand bones around his scorched heart.
His Moon-scarred skin is sick with boils and warts.
His grey beard stinks with goat-shit, sweat, and coal.
20 Fire and heated dust have rawed his eyes to redness;
They hit like iron bullets in my guts.
No kindness in him: the long whip smashes on the donkey like on iron.
The black and brittle coal has clogged his chest with dirt,
The black fragrance of the coal is killing him.

25 He is useful still. I shake with pain to see him pass.
   He has not lost his hating yet, there's that sweet thing to say,
   He farts at the beauty of the raindipped moon.
   The smooth men in their livery of success
   He curses in his killing heart
30 And yearns for thorns to tear their ease.
   His spit blazes in the sun. An emperor's bracelet shines.

Ian McDonald
b. TRINIDAD 1933

The Washerwomen

Down where the river beats itself against the stones
And washes them in clouds of frothy spray,
Or foaming fumbles through them with the thousand tones
Of an orchestra,
5 The women wash, and humming keep a sort of time;
And families of bubbles frisk and float away
To be destroyed,
Like all the baffled hopes that had their little suns,
Tossed on the furious drifts of disappointments.
10 But all the tide
Cradles these clinging bubbles ever still, alike
The friendly little hopes that never leave the heart.

In this big hall of rushing waters women wash
And with the sound of washing,
15 With the steady heaving of their slender shoulders
As they rub their stubborn rags upon the boulders,
They keep a sort of time

With their thoughts. These were unchanging
Like the persistent music here,
20 Of swirling waters,
The crash of wet clothes beaten on the stones,
The sound of wind in leaves,
Or frog croaks after dusk, and the low moan
Of the big sea fighting the river's mouth.

25 The ever changing patterns in the clouds
Before their dissolution into rain;
Or the gay butterflies manoeuvering
Among the leafy camouflage that clothes the banks
And hides their spent remains when they collapse and die,
30 Are symbols of their hopes and gaudy plans
Which once they dreamt. But finally they learn to hope
And make plans less elaborate.
It was the same
With those that washed before them here
35 And passed leaving the soap-stained stones
Where others now half stoop like devotees
To pagan gods.

They have resigned themselves to daylong swishing
Of wet cloth chafing the very stone;
40 And the big symphony of waters rushing
Past clumps of tall stems standing alone,
Apart, like band-leaders, or sentinels,
They must hear the heavy hum
Of wings of insects overgrown,
45 Cleaving the air like bombers on a plotted course.
They must hear the long 'hush' of the wind in leaves
As dead ones flutter down like living things
Until the shadows come.

Owen Campbell
b. ST. VINCENT

The Castaways

The vivid grass with visible delight
Springing triumphant from the pregnant earth,
The butterflies, and sparrows in brief flight
Dancing and chirping for the season's birth,
5 The dandelions and rare daffodils
That touch the deep-stirred heart with hands of gold,

The thrushes sending forth their joyous trills, –
Not these, not these did I at first behold!
But seated on the benches daubed with green,
10 The castaways of life, a few asleep,
Some withered women desolate and mean,
And over all, life's shadows dark and deep.
Moaning I turned away, for misery
I have the strength to bear but not to see.

Claude McKay
b. JAMAICA 1889

Albert

Albert dead Tuesday gone.
They say liver kill him. Liver should live!
Perhaps they say liquor and I hear wrong
for I never see any man take up waters
5 like Albert.

              Today the burial.
Well sir The Society give of the best,
Miss Vi see to that, never mind she harass him
every God-day, everything correct,
10 and Albert shave, and dress so-till;
same Albert who scorn soap, and wear pant
till they have more patch than pant foot;
and the hearse big as Governor car
full up of flowers like Hope Garden—
15 for Albert who never own even a cycle in life,
walk everywhere, and bleed forty-chain to reach hospital,
Albert who never know buttercup from ram-goat rose.

A. L. Hendriks
b. JAMAICA 1922

Ode to Brother Joe

Nothing can soak
Brother Joe's tough sermon,
his head swollen
with certainties

5   When he lights up a s'liff
you can't stop him,
and the door to God, usually shut,
gives in a rainbow gust.

Then it's time for the pipe,
10   which is filled with its water base
and handed to him for his blessing.
He bends over the stem,
goes into the long grace,
and the drums start

15   *the drums start*
Hail Selassie I
Jah Rastafari,
and the room fills with the power
and beauty of blackness,
20   a furnace of optimism.

But the law thinks different.
This evening the Babylon catch
Brother Joe in his act of praise
and carry him off to the workhouse.

25   Who'll save Brother Joe? Hail
Selassie is far away
and couldn't care less,
and the promised ship

is a million light years
30   from Freeport.
But the drums in the tenement house
are sadder than usual tonight

and the brothers suck hard
at their s'liffs and pipes:
35 Before the night's over
Brother Joe has become a martyr;
But still in jail;
And only his woman
who appreciates his humanness more
40 will deny herself of the weed tonight
to hire a lawyer
and put up a true fight.

Meantime, in the musty cell,
Joe invokes, almost from habit,
45 the magic words:
Hail Selassie I
Jah Rastafari,
But the door is real and remains shut.

Anthony McNeill
b. JAMAICA 1941

Squatter's Rites

Peas, corn, potatoes; he had
planted himself
king of a drowsy hill; no one
cared how he came to
5 such green dignity,
scratching his majesty
among the placid chickens.

But after a time, after
his deposition, the uncivil wind
10 snarled anarchy through that
small kingdom. Trees, wild birds

troubled the window,
as though to replace the fowl
that wandered and died of summer;
15 spiders locked the door,
threading the shuddered moths,
and stabbed their twilight needles through
that grey republic. The parliament of dreams
dissolved. The shadows tilted
20 where leaf-white, senatorial lizards
inhabited his chair.

Though one of his sons made it,
blowing reggae (he
dug city life)
25 enough to bury the old Ras
with respect
ability and finally,
a hole in his heart;
and at night when the band played
30 soul, the trumpet
pulse beat
down the hill
to the last post,
abandoned,

35 leaning in its hole
like a sceptre
among the peas, corn, potatoes.

Dennis Scott
b. JAMAICA 1939

Me Cyaan Believe It

Me seh me cyaan believe it
me seh me cyaan believe it

Room dem a rent
me apply widin
5 but as me go een
cockroach rat an scorpion
also come een

Waan good
nose haffi run
10 but me naw go siddung pon high wall
like Humpty Dumpty
me a face me reality

One little bwoy come blow im horn
an me look pon im wid scorn
15 an me realize how me five bwoy-picni
was a victim of de trick
dem call partisan politricks

an me ban me belly
an me bawl
20 an me ban me belly
an me bawl
Lawd
me cyaan believe it
me seh me cyaan believe it

25 Me daughter bwoy-frien name Sailor
an im pass through de port like a ship
more gran-picni fi feed
an de whole a we in need
what a night what a plight
30 an we cyaan get a bite
me life is a stiff fight
an me cyaan believe it
me seh me cyaan believe it

Sittin on de corner wid me frien
35 talkin bout tings an time
me hear one voice seh
'Who dat?'
Me seh 'A who dat?'
'A who a seh who dat
40 when me a seh who dat?'

When yuh teck a stock
dem lick we dung flat
teet start fly
an big man start cry
45 me seh me cyaan believe it
me seh me cyaan believe it

De odder day
me a pass one yard pon de hill
When me teck a stock me hear
50 'Hey, bwoy!'
'Yes, mam?'
'Hey, bwoy!'
'Yes, mam!'
'Yuh clean up de dawg shit?'
55 'Yes, mam.'

An me cyaan believe it
me seh me cyaan believe it

Doris a modder of four
get a wuk as a domestic
60 Boss man move een
an bap si kaisico she pregnant again
bap si kaisico she pregnant again
an me cyaan believe it
me seh me cyaan believe it

65 Deh a yard de odder night
when me hear 'Fire! Fire!'
'Fire, to plate claat!'

Who dead? You dead!
Who dead? Me dead!
70   Who dead? Harry dead!
Who dead? Eleven dead!
Woeeeeeeee
Orange Street fire
deh pon me head
75   an me cyaan believe it
me seh me cyaan believe it

Lawd
me see some blackbud
livin inna one buildin
80   but no rent no pay
so dem cyaan stay
Lawd
de oppress an de dispossess
cyaan get no res

85   What nex?

Teck a trip from Kingston
to Jamaica
Teck twelve from a dozen
an me see me mumma in heaven
90   Madhouse! Madhouse!

Me seh me cyaan believe it
me seh me cyaan believe it

Yuh believe it?
How yuh fi believe it
95   when yuh laugh
an yuh blind yuh eye to it?

But me know yuh believe it
Lawwwwwwwwwwd
me know yuh believe it

Michael Smith
b. JAMAICA 1954 d. 1983

Ad. for a Housing Scheme

Packed tightly like
sums. Their sheer
geometrical lines oppress
architecturally, appearing
5 disinterested, loveless, same.

People who drive past these houses
see them as stacked
-up z –
ros to be quickly got through;
10 accelerate, almost
by instinct, to have them
behind their tail pipes
like bad dreams or carcases.

. Mine, positioned
15 in from the highway, assails
few sensitive motorists, but I,
walking toward its box-
shape this twilight,
see it as part
20 of a huge, grotesque tenement: my house
is ugly for being anonymous.

And now suddenly
the gray, uniform buildings
intersect like years. Poised
25 only for home, I cross
into a harsh, formularized future
where houses and people
flash smally and strictly alike.

Anthony McNeill
b. JAMAICA 1941

University of Hunger

is the university of hunger the wide waste.
is the pilgrimage of man the long march.
The print of hunger wanders in the land.
The green tree bends above the long forgotten.
5   The plains of life rise up and fall in spasms.
The huts of men are fused in misery.

They come treading in the hoofmarks of the mule
passing the ancient bridge
the grave of pride
10   the sudden flight
the terror and the time.

They come from the distant village of the flood
passing from middle air to middle earth
in the common hours of nakedness.

15   Twin bars of hunger mark their metal brows
twin seasons mock them
parching drought and flood.

is the dark ones
the half sunken in the land.
20   is they who had no voice in the emptiness
in the unbelievable
in the shadowless.

They come treading on the mud floor of the year
mingling with dark heavy waters
25   and the sea sound of the eyeless flitting bat.
O long is the march of men and long is the life
and wide is the span.

is air dust and the long distance of memory
is the hour of rain when sleepless toads are silent
30   is broken chimneys smokeless in the wind
is brown trash huts and jagged mounds of iron.

They come in long lines toward the broad city
is the golden moon like a big coin in the sky
is the floor of bone beneath the floor of flesh
35 is the beak of sickness breaking on the stone
O long is the march of men and long is the life
and wide is the span
O cold is the cruel wind blowing.
O cold is the hoe in the ground.

40 They come like sea birds
flapping in the wake of a boat
is the torture of sunset in purple bandages
is the powder of fire spread like dust in the twilight
is the water melodies of white foam on wrinkled sand.

45 The long streets of night move up and down
baring the thighs of a woman
and the cavern of generation.
. The beating drum returns and dies away.
The bearded men fall down and go to sleep.
50 The cocks of dawn stand up and crow like bugles.

is they who rose early in the morning
watching the moon die in the dawn.
is they who heard the shell blow and the iron clang.
is they who had no voice in the emptiness
55 in the unbelievable
in the shadowless.
O long is the march of men and long is the life
and wide is the span.

Martin Carter
b. GUYANA 1927

from **The Dust**

Yuh does get up, walk 'bout,
praise God that yuh body
int turnin' to stone,

an' that you bubbies still big;
5   that you got a good
voice that can shout

for heaven to hear
you: int got nothin' to fear
from no man. You does come

10   to the shop, stop, talk
little bit, get despatch
an' go home;

you still got a back that kin dig
in the fields
15   an' hoe an' pull up the weeds

from the peeny brown
square that you callin' your own;
you int sick an' you children strong;

ev'ry day you see the sun
20   rise, the sun
set; God sen' ev'ry month

a new moon. Dry season
follow wet season again
an' the green crop follow the rain.

25   An' then suddenly so
widdout rhyme
widdout reason

you crops start to die
you can't even see the sun in the sky;
30   an' suddenly so, without rhyme,

without reason, all you hope gone
ev'rything look like it comin' out wrong.
Why is that? What it mean?

Edward Brathwaite
b. BARBADOS 1930

Homestead

Seven splendid cedars break the trades
from the thin gables of my house,
seven towers of song when the trades rage
through their full green season foliage.
5 but weathers veer, the drought returns,
the sun burns emerald to ochre
and thirsty winds strip the boughs bare,
then they are tragic stands of sticks
pitiful in pitiless noons
10 and wear dusk's buskin and the moon's.

And north beyond them lie the fields
which one man laboured his life's days,
one man wearying his bone
shaped them as monuments in stone,
15 hammered them with iron will
and a rugged earthy courage,
and going, left me heritage.
is labour lovely for a man
that drags him daily into earth
20 returns no fragrance of him forth?

The man is dead but I recall
him in my voluntary verse,
his life was unadorned as bread,
he reckoned weathers in his head
25 and wore their ages on his face
and felt their keenness to his bone
the sting of sun and whip of rain.
he read day's event from the dawn
and saw the quality of morning
30 through the sunset mask of evening.

In the fervour of my song
I hold him firm upon the fields
in many homely images.
His ghost's as tall as the tall trees;

35   he tramps these tracks his business made
     by daily roundabout in boots
     tougher and earthier than roots;
     and every furrow of the earth
     and every shaken grace of grass
40   knows him the spirit of the place.

     He was a slave's son, peasant born,
     paisan, paisano – those common
     men about their fields, world over,
     of sugar, cotton, corn or clover
45   who are unsung but who remain
     perpetual as the passing wind,
     unkillable as the frail grass;
     who, from their graves within their graves,
     nourish the splendour of the earth
50   and give her substance, give her worth.

     Poets and artists turn again,
     construct your cunning tapestries
     upon the ages of their acres,
     the endless labours of their years;
55   still at the centre of their world
     cultivate the first green graces,
     courage, strength and kindliness,
     love of man and beast and landscape;
     still sow and graft the primal good,
60   green boughs of innocence to God.

E. M. Roach
b. TOBAGO 1915 d. 1974

Husks

Legs tucked, pressed
into the strict undercarriage,
they circle the air
in full-cognizance of its drifts and secrets.

5 Each sneaks out a loft
and settles upon it,
straddling it till the wings laze wide and relax,
content with this slow, effortless round and descent.

Cunning, they all assume
10 a careless carnival spirit,
less vultures than children
spinning harmlessly round the under-sky's axis

They are dangerous, nevertheless.
Their starved eyes, endlessly seeking,
15 relentlessly reconnoiter our steppes.
At the first proof of death

that charming balance disrupts,
and the crows, cropped into dread
fallen angels, crash down and rip
20 at our leavings till nothing is left.

Then they are off, flap-
ping back fat
but still famished,
in an ache for more servings from death,

25 Hungering home from the husks of the spirit.

Anthony McNeill
b. JAMAICA 1941

Growing Up

Bird

That day the bird hunted an empty, gleaming sky
and climbed and coiled and spun measures of joy,
half-sleeping in the sly wind way
above my friend and me. Oh,
5   its wings' wind-flick and fleche were free
and easy in the sun, and a whip's tip
tracing of pleasure its mute madrigal,
that I below watched it so tall
it could not fall save slow
10 down the slow day.

'What is it?' said my friend
'Yonder. . . .'
          Hill and home patterned and curved
and frozen in the white round air
15 'Yes, there,' he said, 'I see it–'

              Up
the steep sky till the eye
lidded from weight of sun on earth and wing!

'Watch this,' he said, bending for stones,
20 and my boy's throat grew tight with warning
to the bird that rode the feathered morning.

'Now there's a good shot, boy!' he said.
I was only ten then.
'If you see any more be sure to shout
25 but don't look at the sun too long,' he said,
'makes your eyes run.'

Dennis Scott
b. JAMAICA 1939

Flowers

I have never learnt the names of flowers.
From beginning, my world has been a place
Of pot-holed streets where thick, sluggish gutters race
In slow time, away from garbage heaps and sewers
5 Past blanched old houses around which cowers
Stagnant earth. There, scarce green thing grew to chase
The dull-grey squalor of sick dust; no trace
Of plant save few sparse weeds; just these, no flowers.

One day they cleared a space and made a park
10 There in the city's slums; and suddenly
Came stark glory like lightning in the dark,
While perfume and bright petals thundered slowly.
I learnt no names, but hue, shape and scent mark
My mind, even now, with symbols holy.

Dennis Craig
b. GUYANA 1929

The Pond

There was this pond in the village
and little boys, he heard till he was sick,
were not allowed too near.
Unfathomable pool, they said,
5 that swallowed men and animals just so;
and in its depths, old people said,
swam galliwasps and nameless horrors;
bright boys kept away.

Though drawn so hard by prohibitions,
10 the small boy, fixed in fear, kept off;
till one wet summer, grass growing lush,
paths muddy, slippery, he found himself
there, at the fabled edge.

The brooding pond was dark.
15 Sudden, escaping cloud, the sun
came bright; and, shimmering in guilt,
he saw his own face peering from the pool.

Mervyn Morris
b. JAMAICA 1937

Pa

In the quiet of the dining-room
an ageing man sits huddled over scrambled eggs;
a copy of the *Guardian* drooling from his hands.

And in the silent rage of his broken posture,
5   he concludes how seldom he laughed in those years when
he had
sharp two-toned shoes, double-breasted suits and
steady hands.
Blanks circle him;
10 and yet those days when he rolled and pitched
the seas with the best, are a memory away.

He muses how committed he was to the corner stones
of his world. Rocks that once supported a fixed drive.
He scrambles for his thoughts across the headlines

15 recounts on stubby fingers the vices he declined
the strain of sacrifice his children never held.

... But dazed by so much thought and recall
the ageing man keels over. Almost bent double, he's
anchored to his eggs.

Victor Questel
b. TRINIDAD 1949 d. 1982

Ave Maria

From a church across the street
   Children repeat
Hail Mary, full of Grace.
   Skipping the syllables; Follow-the-leader pace.

5 A little girl, (the Lord is with thee,)
   White in organdy,
Lifts her starched, black face
   Towards the barricaded altar
Meadowed in lace.

10 (Blessed art Thou among women.)
   Her child's fingers rove the coloured beads
One after one.
   (Blessed is the fruit of Thy womb, –)
Yea; and blessed, too.
15 Ripe fruit on trees, window-close,
Under a tropical sun.

Bend low the laden bough
   Child-high; sweeten her incense-laden breath
With food, good Mary. (Holy Mary, Mother of God,
20 Pray for us sinners.) And for the blameless,
Now, before the hour of their death.

Barbara Ferland
b. JAMAICA 1919

Thinking Back on Yard Time

We swim in the mooneye.
The girls brown breasts float.
Sea sways against sandbanks.

We all frogkick water.
5 Palm trees stand there watching
with limbs dark like our crowd.

We porpoise-dive, we rise,
we dog-shake water from our heads.
Somebody swims on somebody.

10 We laugh, we dry ourselves.
Sea-rolling makes thunder
around coast walls of cliffs.

Noise at Square is rum-talk
from the sweaty rum bar
15 without one woman's word.

Skylarking, in our seizure,
in youthful bantering,
we are lost in togetherness.

Our road isn't dark tonight.
20 Trees – mango, breadfruit – all,
only make own shapely shadow.

Moon lights up pastureland.
Cows, jackass, all, graze quietly.
We are the cackling party.

James Berry
b. JAMAICA 1924

Roots

Who danced Saturday mornings
Between immortelle roots,
And played about his palate
The mellowness of cocoa beans.
5 Who felt the hint of the cool river,
In his blood,
The hint of the cool river
Chill and sweet.

Who followed curved shores
10 Between two seasons.
Who took stones in his hands
Stones white as milk.
Examining the island in his hands;
And shells,
15 Shells as pink as frog's eyes
From the sea.

Who saw the young corn sprout
With April rain.
Who measured the young meaning
20 By looking at the moon.
And walked roads a footpath's width,
And calling,
Cooed with mountain doves
Come morning time.

25 Who breathed mango odour
From his polished cheek.
Who followed the cus-cus weeders
In their rich performance.
Who heard the bamboo flute wailing
30 Fluting, wailing,
And watched the poui golden
Listening.

Who with the climbing sinews
Climbed the palm
35 To where the wind plays most,
And saw a chasmed pilgrimage
Making agreement for his clean return.
Whose heaviness
Was heaviness of dreams,
40 From drowsy gifts.

Harold Telemaque
b. TOBAGO 1909

To My Mother

It is not long, not many days are left,
Of the dead sun, nights of the crumbled moon;
Nor far to go; not all your roads of growth,
Love, grief, labour of birth and bone
5 And the slow slope from the blood's noon
Are shorter than this last.

And it is nothing. Only the lusty heroes
And those whose summer's sweet with lust
And wine and roses fear. The children do not;
10 Theirs is young Adam's innocence.
The old do not; they welcome the earth's suction
And the bone's extinction into rock.

The image of your beauty growing green,
Your bone's adolescence I could not know,
15 Come of your middle years, your July loins.
I found you strong and tough as guava scrub,
Hoeing the ground, reaping the ripe corn;
Kneading and thumping the thick dough for bread.

And now you're bowed, bent over to the ground;
20 An old gnarled tree, all her boughs drooped
Upon the cross of death, you crawl up
Your broken stairs like Golgotha, and dead bones
Clutch at your dying bones . . .

I do not mourn, but all my love
25 Praise life's revival through the eternal year.
I see death broken at each seed's rebirth.
My poems labour from your blood
As all my mind burns on our peasant stock
That cannot be consumed till time is killed.

30 Oh, time's run past the time your hands made bread
To this decrepitude; but in the stream
Of time I watch the stone, the image
Of my mother making bread my boyhood long,
Mossed by the crusty memories of bread.
35 O may my art grow whole as her hands' craft.

Eric Roach
b. TRINIDAD 1915 d. 1974

Encounters

Revelation

Turn sideways now and let them see
What loveliness escapes the schools,
Then turn again, and smile, and be
The perfect answer to those fools
5 Who always prate of Greece and Rome,
'The face that launched a thousand ships',
And suchlike things, but keep tight lips
For burnished beauty nearer home.
Turn in the sun, my love, my love!
10 What palm-like grace! What poise! I swear
I prize these dusky limbs above my life.
What laughing eyes! What gleaming hair!

H. A. Vaughan
b. SANTO DOMINGO 1901

Caribbean Journal

He stands outside the fencing looking in.

Inside sunbathers relishing their flesh—
some white, some black, and some of other skins—
diving and swimming feign not to notice him,
5 fingers of doubt spread wide, gripping the holes of mesh.

Some people on the grass are picknicking.

His pants are torn; he does not have a shirt;
his face, a mask of sun-flaked grease and dirt
too young to understand his day's events,
10   dreams mountain-slide of magic dollars and cents
to cancel knowledge of the stomach's pain,
eyes learning what will later reach his brain.

In time they'll be afraid to hear his curse
at god's unholy sunday-school arrangement,
15   put him inside a wire mesh, or worse,
and sunbathe in the same sun on his hearse
or perish if his bullet gets them first.

Cecil Gray
b. TRINIDAD 1923

Earth is Brown

Earth is brown and rice is green,
And air is cold on the face of the soul

Oh grandfather, my grandfather,
your dhoti is become a shroud
5   your straight hair a curse
in this land where
rice no longer fills the belly
or the empty placelessness
of your soul.

10   For you cannot remember India.
The passage of time
has too long been trampled over
to bear your wistful recollections,
and you only know the name
15   of the ship they brought you on
because your daadi told it to you.

Your sons with their city faces
don't know it at all
Don't want to know it.
20 Nor to understand that
you cannot cease
this communion with the smell
of cow-dung at fore-day morning,
or the rustling wail
25 of yellow-green rice
or the security of
mud between your toes
or the sensual pouring
of paddy through your fingers.

30 Oh grandfather, my grandfather,
your dhoti is become a shroud.
Rice beds no longer call your sons.
They are clerks in the city of streets
Where life is a weekly paypacket
35 purchasing identity in Tiger Bay,
seeking a tomorrow in today's unreality.

You are too old now to doubt
that Hannuman hears you.
Yet outside your logie
40 the fluttering cane
flaps like a plaintive tabla
in the wind.
And when the spaces inside you
can no longer be filled
45 by the rank beds of rice,
and the lowing morning
cannot stir you to rise
from your ghoola,
The music in your heart
50 will sound a rustling sound,
and the bamboos to Hannuman
will be a sitar in the wind.

Shana Yardan
b. GUYANA 1942

The Saddhu of Couva

For Kenneth Ramchand

When sunset, a brass gong,
vibrate through Couva,
is then I see my soul, swiftly unsheathed,
like a white cattle bird growing more small
5   over the ocean of the evening canes,
and I sit quiet, waiting for it to return
like a hog-cattle blistered with mud,
because, for my spirit, India is too far.
And to that gong
10 sometimes bald clouds in saffron robes assemble
sacred to the evening,
sacred even to Ramlochan,
singing Indian hits from his jute hammock
while evening strokes the flanks
15 and silver horns of his maroon taxi,
as the mosquitoes whine their evening mantras,
my friend Anopheles, on the sitar,
and the fireflies making every dusk Divali.

I knot my head with a cloud,
20 my white mustache bristle like horns,
my hands are brittle as the pages of Ramayana.
Once the sacred monkeys multiplied like branches
in the ancient temples; I did not miss them,
because these fields sang of Bengal,
25 behind Ramlochan Repairs there was Uttar Pradesh;
but time roars in my ears like a river,
old age is a conflagration
as fierce as the cane fires of crop time.
I will pass through these people like a cloud,
30 they will see a white bird beating the evening sea
of the canes behind Couva,
and who will point it as my soul unsheathed?
Neither the bridegroom in beads,
nor the bride in her veils,
35 their sacred language on the cinema hoardings.

I talked too damn much on the Couva Village Council.
I talked too softly, I was always drowned
by the loudspeakers in front of the stores
or the loudspeakers with the greatest pictures.
40 I am best suited to stalk like a white cattle bird
on legs like sticks, with sticking to the Path
between the canes on a district road at dusk.
Playing the Elder. There are no more elders.
Is only old people.

45 My friends spit on the government.
I do not think is just the government.
Suppose all the gods too old,
Suppose they dead and they burning them,
supposing when some cane cutter
50 start chopping up snakes with a cutlass
he is severing the snake-armed god,
and suppose some hunter has caught
Hanuman in his mischief in a monkey cage.
Suppose all the gods were killed by electric light?

55 Sunset, a bonfire, roars in my ears;
embers of blown swallows dart and cry,
like women distracted,
around its cremation.
I ascend to my bed of sweet sandalwood.

Derek Walcott
b. ST. LUCIA 1930

Tizzic

For he was a slave
to drums, to flutes, brave

brass and rhythm; the jump-up saved
him from the thought of holes, damp,

5   rain through the roof of his have-
nothing cottage; kele, kalinda-stamp,

the limbo, calypso-season camp,
these he loved best of all; the road-march tramp

down Princess Street, round Mar-
10   aval; Kitch, Sparrow, Dougla, these were the stars

of his melodic heaven. Their little winking songs car-
ried him back to days of green unhur-

ried growing. The Car-
nival's apotheosis blazed for two nights

15   without fear or sorrow, colour bar
or anyone to question or restrain his height-

ened, borrowed glory. He walked so far
on stilts of song, of masqueraded story; stars

were near. Doors of St. Peter's heaven were ajar.
20   Mary, Christ's Christmas mother was there

too, her sweet inclined compassion
in full view. In such bright swinging company

he could no longer feel the cramp
of poverty's confinement, spirit's damp;

25 he could have all he wished, he ever
    wanted. But the good stilts splinter-

    ed, wood legs broke, calypso steel pan
    rhythm faltered. The midnight church

    bell fell across the glow, the lurch-
30 ing cardboard crosses. Behind the masks, grave

    Lenten sorrows waited: Ash-
    Wednesday, ashes, darkness, death.

    After the *bambalula bambulai*
    he was a slave again.

                              Edward Brathwaite
                              b. BARBADOS 1930

Lines Written on a Train

    If, in response to the sobbing
    Of wheels consuming miles of rail
    Or the spirituals the peasants sing,
    My heart were to flutter and reel

5   And my eyes to fill with tears,
    He would not understand who sits
    At my side and silently shares
    The display of commonplace sights:

    The fields where restless fires
10 Cause a horse to break his rope
    And flee, erratic, through the choirs
    That moving sing and singing reap

The canes; for mine and mine alone
Is the thought, that through the peasants' hearts –
15   Though they seem as callous as stone –
Some river runs which soothes their hurts,

While willy-nilly hearts like mine
Must roam ten thousand years of days
Afraid, lest with intractable whine
20   The river absorb the fire that slowly dies.

Cecil Herbert
b. TRINIDAD 1926

Country

It is in the raw country that we come upon ourselves.
   Here the hoe-man is no rejecter of heaven,
And people wriggle their toes in the mud
And say:
5   Something for all of us here,
Come dig, time to plant up.

These people have never seen
Blood spilled over the charmed penny.

These people have never been
10   Where smoke is a law
And they persecute you with pen and ink
And most folks are sad
Because they have found out about things.

Raw, we say.

15   It is in the crude country that we come upon ourselves.

E. McG. Keane
b. ST. VINCENT 1927

Limbo Dancer at Immigration

It was always the same
at every border/at every frontier/
at every port/at every airport/
                     of every metropolis

5   The same hassle
from authorities

the same battle
with bureaucrats

a bunch of official cats
10 ready to scratch

looking limbo dancer up & down
scrutinizing passport with a frown

COUNTRY OF ORIGIN: SLAVESHIP

Never heard of that one
15 the authorities sniggered

Suppose you got here on a banana boat
the authorities sniggered

More likely a spaceship
the authorities sniggered

20 Slaveship/spaceship/Pan Am/British Airways/Air France
It's all the same
smiled limbo dancer

Now don't give us any of your lip
the authorities sniggered

25 ANY IDENTIFYING MARKS?

And when limbo dancer showed them sparks
of vision in eyes that held rivers
                    it meant nothing to them

And when limbo dancer held up hands
30 that told a tale of nails
                    it meant nothing to them

And when limbo dancer offered a neck
that bore the brunt of countless lynchings
                    it meant nothing to them

35 And when limbo dancer revealed ankles
bruised with the memory of chains
                    it meant nothing to them

So limbo dancer bent over backwards
                    & danced
                    & danced
                    & danced

until from every limb
flowed a trail of red

& what the authorities thought
45 was a trail of blood

was only spilt duty-free wine

so limbo dancer smiled
saying I have nothing to declare

& to the sound of drum disappeared

John Agard
b. GUYANA 1930

Men and Women

In Absence

What golden years were visioned for her sake
She must not know, nor what delights were planned;
She must not know what joys have fled the land
To mark her absence, nor what longings make
5   This dull month still more leaden, nor what ache
Now burdens singing. Silence must withstand
Her cold forgetfulness, and Love's own hand
Must write this vow although his proud heart break.
And so no wail, no tears, no wish, no sigh
10   Must come from him. Silence alone is meet.
For he must rise above remembered things
As common men fix tyrants with their eye
And failing, try to tower in defeat,
And captive, still acquire the air of kings.

H. A. Vaughan
b. SANTO DOMINGO 1901

Family Pictures

In spite of love
desire to be alone
haunts him like prophecy.

Observe: the baby chuckles,
5 gurgles his delight
that daddy-man is handy,
to be stared at, clawed at,
spitted-up upon,
the baby's elder brother
10 laughs, or hugs, and nags
for popcorn or a pencil
or a trip.

And see: the frazzled wife
who jealously
15 protects the idol infant
from the smallest chance
of harm, and anxious
in the middle of the night
wakes up to coughs; and checks,
20 and loves, and screams
her nerves; but loves him
patient still: the wife
who sweets the bigger boy
and teases him through homework,
25 bright as play.

But you may not observe
(it is a private sanctuary)
the steady glowing power
that makes a man feel loved,
30 feel needed, all of time;
yet frees him, king of her
emotions, jockey of her
flesh, to cherish
his own corner
35 of the cage.

In spite of love
this dream:
to go alone
to where
40   the fishing boats are empty
on the beach
and no one knows
which man is
father, husband, victim,
45   king, the master of one cage.

Mervyn Morris
b. JAMAICA 1937

Birthday Honours

Your birthday; so I sit
Cudgelling the brain for tunes to whistle,
Pondering love and anniversaries.

So many perfect poems have lied
5   Of love sublime or love decaying or dead.
Though your man Donne, thinking his way to truth,
Moulds spirit and senses into sinewy lines
Wriggling their honesty to life,
Yet even he must lie, forcing a form
10   Where no form is, tidying
Where order is untrue.
Love is a theme for prose.

But on your birthday let me shape a poem:
Good lies may testify of love.

15 Your fullest year has withered in a night.
'The page is turned' or 'Time has dug a tomb,
The months and minutes buried in its depths,
Silent beyond recall.'
'What fools we are who must fragment
20 The long continuous string of time!
Birthdays are only knots, the small reminders
That time will stop, that human beauty fades.'
'Birthdays are the firm consoling corners
In the long dark echoing room of time.'

25 Time is a lie, the past is now
And all our futures are our present minutes;
There is no string of time, neatly unravelling
Its agelong progress till the end is cut,
Only a dark pool swirling with living moments,
30 Love-letters, matches, galliwasps,
Empty old toothpaste-tubes and railway-tickets,
Markers that flow from my time into yours,
Ours into others', others' into ours,
For all our times are one, the pool's confusion
35 Is falsified by cuckoo-clocks and calendars.

Thus wildly I celebrate my birthday singing yours;
Loving, I swear that love in art is lies;
And, wanting art, must swear that art is falsehood;
And in the whirlpool, clutching at straws,
40 Must pray through love and art
That something I can do may outlive time.

Mervyn Morris
b. JAMAICA 1937

Philpot Puzzled

'There's someone else,' she says,
sitting opposite him tracing

with a finger too elegant
for his wife, patterns on the oilskin.

5   She is speaking, not to or at Philpot
not even *through* him, but slightly

over his shoulder; and the sentence
comes from someone other than Maureen.

'There's someone else,' is a guest
10   in the house replacing her, discarding

her life's '*A goin' dance wid Roy.*
Expec' me when you see me' language.

He's afraid to touch the newly-
elegant finger which is not hers;

15   and searches for a suitable phrase
of submission to match his new status.

But it doesn't come. He is still
pondering, alone at the table, giving

the impression of a defeated Philpot
20   who doesn't care.

E. A. Markham
b. MONTSERRAT 1941

Anna

Still dreamt of, still missed,
especially on raw, rainy mornings, your face shifts
into anonymous schoolgirl faces, a punishment,
since sometimes, you condescend to smile,
5   since at the corners of the smile there is forgiveness.

Besieged by sisters, you were a prize
of which they were too proud, circled
by the thorn thicket of their accusation,
what grave deep wrong, what wound have you brought Anna?

10   The rain season comes with its load.
The half-year has travelled far. Its back hurts.
It drizzles wearily.

It is twenty years since,
after another war, the shell-cases are where?
15   But in our brassy season, our imitation autumn,
your hair puts out its fire,
your gaze haunts innumerable photographs,

now clear, now indistinct,
all that pursuing generality,
20   that vengeful conspiracy with nature,

all that sly informing of objects,
and behind every line, your laugh
frozen into a lifeless photograph.

In that hair I could walk through the wheatfields of Russia,
25   your arms were downed and ripening pears,
for you became, in fact, another country,

you are Anna of the wheatfield and the weir,
you are Anna of the solid winter rain,
Anna of the smoky platform and the cold train,
30   in that war of absence, Anna of the steaming stations,

gone from the marsh-edge,
from the drizzled shallows
puckering with gooseflesh,
Anna of the first green poems that startingly hardened,

35   of the mellowing breasts now,
Anna of the lurching, long flamingoes
of the harsh salt lingering in the thimble
of the bather's smile,

Anna of the darkened house, among the reeking shell-cases
40   lifting my hand and swearing us to her breast,
unbearably clear-eyed.

You are all Annas, enduring all goodbyes,
within the cynical station of your body,
Christie, Karenina, big-boned and passive,

45   that I found life within some novel's leaves
more real than you, already chosen
as his doomed heroine. You knew, you knew.

Derek Walcott
b. ST. LUCIA 1930

Notes on a September Day

A nightingale hangs upside
down, its body death-
pinned to the livewire.

Was it he that sang
5   from the otaheite
shaped like a fir

who nested hooded
amid the high branches
tame enough not to fly off

10 when the children scraped
the lean season for fruit?
Once, after the rain,

he stirred such a storm of music
it seemed the tree itself sang.
15 The season is done;

The apples which hung
like Christmas decorations
are gone

back into the ground;
20 tattered kite-tails swing
back and forth from the wires,

flayed by the wind;
The shocked nightingale hangs
stiff and inverted:

25 Between kisses
I feel your seasonal body
stiffen in rigor mortis.

Anthony McNeill
b. JAMAICA 1941

Drought

The woman is barren. And the blackbirds
have had a hard time this year with the drought
and fallen like moths to the field's floor.

The woman is barren. And the city,
5 crawling south like an oil-slick,
will soon be around her ankles.

So she sings: 'Will you marry me?
I will go searching under many flat stones
for moisture of the departed rains.'

10 Sings: 'O World, will you marry me?'

The riverbed's dried up completely, the lizards
have taken to the trees, to the high branches.
The cane rolls westwards, burning burning

In the sunset of her time, in the ploughed crater
15 where the woman like a frail apostrophe
dances palely each evening

Among the fallen blackbirds.

Wayne Brown
b. TRINIDAD 1944

Being a Woman

Poem for Mothers

Strong women,
glueing together
families for absent fathers.
Surrogate dads,
5 who soothe and rear
your children while
your man absconds —
To yet another woman
to be left alone.
10 Bearing and rearing
his careless seed.
And yet,
our weakness and our pride
go hand in hand,
15 with anger —
to their beds.
And so it goes.
Lives fragmented with giving,
and being taken.

20 And so one night
Thursday, Saturday or whatever,
a sister kills or self destructs;
While huddled in our hopelessness,
I wait my turn.

Cheryl Albury
b. EXUMA 1944

Superwife

Did you see her?
That damned
mouthing robot.
High on detergents, cleaners,
5   husband's socks
and children's knickers.
DID YOU SEE HER?
Damned programmed
idiot in a dolly's body.
10   Priming, preening, plastering
her brain and soul
with the virtues of giving.

DID YOU SEE HER,
my friend?
15   Today she was at her best.
(or worst, some say)
Today's the day
they strapped and carted her away.

Cheryl Albury
b. EXUMA 1944

Old I

If I get old,
I want to sit near the water
in flour bag drawers.
My lumpy stretch marked legs
5   causing rivulets
where sand gives way to sea
bathing myself.
My naked flabby breasts,
my navel secreted in limp dead skin,
10   dipping sea water
with an enamel cup,
throwing it over my head
and cussing anyone who stares.

Dionne Brand
b. TRINIDAD 1953

Old II

If I get old,
hell with them people,
they better not bother me anymore
'cause I'll do something old and crazy,
5   like spit through my gums in their faces,
they better not mess with me
'cause I've got some shabby secrets
like who I saw with his hand in my blood.
They better leave me alone then,
10   pretend I'm mad!
'cause I've got some rattling stories.

Dionne Brand
b. TRINIDAD 1953

Tell Me

So tell me what you have
to give: I have strong limbs
to make a lap of love
a brow to gaze at in
5   the quiet times half light and
lips for kissing: I'm well
fixed for all love's traffic

And further, I've an ear
open around the clock
10 you know, like those phone
numbers that you call at
anytime. And such soft eyes
that smile and ferret out
the truth. Extraordinary

15 eyes, and gentle – you can see
yourself. It's strong and warm
and dark, this womb I've got
and fertile: you can be
a child and play in
20 there: and if you fall and
hurt yourself, it's easy

to be mended: I know
it sounds a little much
but that's the way it seems
25 to me. So tell me, brother

what have you to give?

Pamela Mordecai
b. JAMAICA 1942

Summer and Kitsilano Beach

The sun has come
to clean the rotting heads
vomited by the retreating tides of winter.

They will be
5 clean scoured skulls;
that finger
will be a flute of whitened bone.

Perhaps that darkhaired girl
wearing sunglasses and yellow slacks
10 will blow it.

She sits on a brown log
with her legs carefully closed.

A man kicks at a shell.
He is looking at the girl
15 from the corners
of his pointed eyes.
If you look hard enough
you can see writhing
slowly toward the girl
20 his tentacles of lust.

Judy Miles
b. TRINIDAD 1944

Lunch Hour

Frederick Street
suffocating,
strangled by people.

Stiletto heels
5 stab at the pavement.

In the formica atmosphere
waiters scuttle by
serving diners their noon portion
of air-conditioned aloofness.

10 Waiting
bites hugely
into the time.

At last at the elbow
a waiter
15 with his 'Instant Coffee' smile.

They've tried to make
that awkward dark cell
below the staircase
into a romantic alcove
20 but
eating there alone
as she always does
the young girl barricades
herself behind a stare
25 hard as old toast.

Going back
the balding city square
smells of dust, detachment
and passions discarded
30 like cheap coats.

Judy Miles
b. TRINIDAD 1944

Crow Poem

I want so much to put
my arms around you but
extended they are feathered
vanes, snapped, tatty things
5   no longer curving.

My voice wants to say things
about blue skies, blond sand,
yet a rasping, carrion croak
jets from my beak
10 sharp edged.

Condemned to live a life for which
I am ill suited, improperly
dressed. Perhaps there is out there
one crow, wheeling over the city dump
15 convinced she is a woman.

Christine Craig
b. JAMAICA

Politics and Society

Mailboat to Hell

Lord, help the mailboat to Hell.
Lord, help the mailboat to Hell.

The mailboat to Hell is filled to the cabin
With souls crying words they don't know
5   Such heavenly cries as Freedom and Justice
And curses for John Statusquo
Ah, but this cut is muddy Lord
This cut is rough
This sea is deep Lord
10 Are words enough?

I'm trapped on the deck of a ship doomed to sink
If the captain don't trust the crew
I'm caught in a swell of the crowd that won't think
But depends on the skill of the few
15 Oh, but the sea is muddy Lord
How trapped I feel
The cut is so dark Lord
And who's at the wheel?

Patrick Rahming
b. NASSAU 1944

This Is The Dark Time, My Love

This is the dark time, my love.
All around the land brown beetles crawl about.
The shining sun is hidden in the sky.
Red flowers bend their heads in awful sorrow.

5 This is the dark time, my love.
It is the season of oppression, dark metal, and tears.
It is the festival of guns, the carnival of misery.
Everywhere the faces of men are strained and anxious.

Who comes walking in the dark night time?
10 Whose boot of steel tramps down the slender grass?
It is the man of death, my love, the stranger invader
watching you sleep and aiming at your dream.

Martin Carter
b. GUYANA 1927

No Man's Land

The body of a fourteen year old caught playing politics
Makes a hummock on the ground beside his ratchet knife
Which drew blood but cannot bleed for him.
The muzzle of a sawn-off shot gun masks the eye of one
Who, being a man (?), thinks himself a great gun.
The gully scrub cannot hide him forever;
Silenced, he drops the gun and becomes a dead man.

Now the killer's 'baby mother' is caught by the press photographer;
For the morning paper and forever she throws up her arms
In the traditional gesture of prayer.
Wai oh! Aie! Eheu! mourns the camera shot matron
Whose stringy son, like a sucked mango seed,
Lies there no more use to anyone;
Soon to be inseparable from the rest of the levelled ground.
Why this pieta needs to be enacted in our land
No one can explain:
It clearly belongs within the pieties of a museum frame.
Is there no way but through this scene?

Gloria Escoffery
b. JAMAICA 1923

To the Unknown Non-Combatant

When the battle started
he was quick to duck.
He lay on his face in the open street
cursing his luck.

5   'Come join us!' (voices from the left)
'Come help us in the fight!'
'Be honest with yourself; you're ours,'
said voices from the right.

Meanwhile the bullets overhead
10 were troubling him somewhat
and buildings burning either side
had made the middle hot.

He thought perhaps he'd better choose.
He crawled to join a side.
15 A bullet clapped him in the neck –
of course he died.

They left him face-down in the dust,
carcass going rotten.
Bullets whistled overhead.
20 He was forgotten.

Mervyn Morris
b. JAMAICA 1937

A White Man Considers the Situati

Perhaps it is time to retreat from these well-loved shores.
The swell heaves on the beach, angry clouds pile:
The surf is ominous, storms are coming.
I see I am a tourist in my own land:
5 My brutal tenancy is over, they all say,
The centuries have faded like a dream...

Every day it is harder for the timid to make plans,
People do not say good morning with the former politeness
The pavements feel safe only when old men pass.
10 The grip of power slides away, slides.
Something is missing in days still filled with pleasure;
There is emptiness, dreaming in the air.
Where ruling ends, the ruler cannot stay:
A diminished mastery is the keenest woe.

15 The best measure is the use of time,
My father's father planted once
A green tree in this quiet garden:
It was to yield ancestral wood
To grace my grandson's christening chair.
20 The best measure is the use of time.

I decorate now my dark-skinnned love
With hibiscus for her shining hair
The petals fade, the sun burns out
Red hibiscus in her shining hair.

25 I lie sleepless in the embroidered sheets,
A sprig of khus-khus scents the room.
The night is dark with cloud, and lonely.
The black sentries are whispering, restless.
My father heard a hurricane of nightingales
30 Once upon a time, once upon a time.
Now the owl hoots, signalling danger coming
The moon is half alight, throwing coldness.

Ian McDonald
b. TRINIDAD 1933

Parades, Parades

There's the wide desert, but no one marches
except in the pads of old caravans,
there is the ocean, but the keels incise
the precise, old parallels,
5   there's the blue sea above the mountains
but they scratch the same lines
in the jet trails,
so the politicians plod
without imagination, circling
10 the same sombre gardens
with its fountain dry in the forecourt,
the gri-gri palms dessicating
dung pods like goats,
the same lines rule the White Papers,
15 the same steps ascend Whitehall,
and only the name of the fool changes
under the plumed white cork-hat
for the Independence Parades
revolving around, in calypso,
20 to the brazen joy of the tubas.

Why are the eyes of the beautiful
and unmarked children
in the uniforms of the country
bewildered and shy,
25 why do they widen in terror
of the pride drummed into their minds?
Were they truer, the old songs,
when the law lived far away,
when the veiled queen, her girth
30 as comfortable as cushions,
upheld the orb with its stern admonitions?
We wait for the changing of statues,
for the change of parades.

Here he comes now, here he comes!
35 Papa! Papa! With his crowd,
the sleek, waddling seals of his Cabinet,
trundling up to the dais,
as the wind puts its tail between
the cleft of the mountain, and a wave
40 coughs once, abruptly.
Who will name this silence
respect? Those forced, hoarse hosannas
awe? That tin-ringing tune
from the pumping, circling horns
45 the New World? Find a name
for that look on the faces
of the electorate. Tell me
how it all happened, and why
I said nothing.

Derek Walcott
b. ST. LUCIA 1930

O Dreams O Destinations

But I returned to find Jack
Kennedy invading Cuba

black riots in Aruba
and Trinidad

5   refusing thirsty US marines water.
For selfishness, when young, played on the floor

with soldiers: the mind's Napoleons with dir-
ty hands;

and selfishness, no
10 longer young, still on

the floor with soldiers:
but now our islands' leaders:

clever caught democracy of laymen preachers,
lawyers, pupil teacher teachers,

15 typists, skilled hospital
porters; each in his Wal-

ter Mitty world a wild Napoleon with dir-
ty hands; each blind

to that harsh light and vision that had once
20 consumed them; eager now, ambitious,

anxious that their single-
minded fames should rise

up uncorrupted from the foundry flames
of time's unblemished brasses, while the

25 supporting poor, famished upon their simple
politics of fish and broken bread,

begin to catch their royal asses,
denuded into silence like the stones

where their shacks sit, which
30 their picks hit, where beaten spirits,

trapped in flesh,
litter the landscape with their broken homes . . .

Edward Brathwaite
b. BARBADOS 1930

Creators

Jaffo the Calypsonian

Jaffo was a great calypsonian, a fire ate up his soul to sing
    and play calypso iron music.

And when he was small he made many-coloured ping-pong
    drums and searched them for the island music.

5   Drums of beaten oil-barrel iron daubed in triangles, with
    stolen paint from a harbour warehouse.

Now he seized the sorrow and the bawdy farce in metal-
    harsh beat and his own thick voice.

10 He was not famous in the tents: he went there once
    and not a stone clapped and he was afraid of respectable
    eyes;
The White-suited or gay-shirted lines of business men or
    tourists muffled his deep urge.

But he went back to the Indian tailor's shop and sung well
15   and to the Chinese and sweepstake shop and sung well,

Unsponsored calypsoes, and in the scrap lots near the Dry
    River lit by one pitch-oil lamp or two

He would pound his ping-pong and sing his hoarse voice out
    for ragged still-eyed men.

20 But in the rumshop he was best, drinking the heavy sweet
    molasses rum he was better than any calypso man;

In front of the rows of dark red bottles, in the cane-scented
    rooms his clogged throat rang and rang with staccato chant.

25   Drunk then, he was best, easier in pain from the cancer in
    his throat but holding the memory of it.

On the rough floors of rum-shops, strewn with bottle-tops
    and silver-headed corks and broken green bottle-glass.

30   He was released from pain into remembered pain, his thick
    voice rose and grated in brassy fear and fierce joke.

His voice beat with bitterness and fun, as if they told of old
    things, hurt ancestral pride and great slave-humour.

He would get a rum if he sang well so perhaps there was
    that of it too –

35   He was always the best, though, he was the best: the ragged
    men said so and the old men.

One month before he died his voice thickened to a hard
    final silence;

The look of unsung calypsoes stared in his eyes, a terrible
40   thing to watch in the rat-trap rum shops.

When he could not stand with pain he was taken in the
    public ward of the Colonial hospital.

Rafeeq, the Indian man who in Marine Square watches the
    birds all day for his God, was there also

45   Later he told about Jaffo in a long mad chant to the rum
    shop men; they laughed at the story.

Until the end Jaffo stole spoons from the harried nurses to
    beat rhythm on his iron bedposts.

Ian McDonald
b. TRINIDAD 1933

Landscape Painter, Jamaica

for Albert Huie

I watch him set up easel,
Both straddling precariously
A corner of the twisted, climbing
Mountain track.

5 A tireless humming-bird, his brush
Dips, darts, hovers now here, now there,
Where puddles of pigment
Bloom in the palette's wild small garden.

The mountains pose for him
10 In a family group –
Dignified, self-conscious, against the wide blue screen
Of morning; low green foot-hills
Sprawl like grandchildren about the knees
Of seated elders. And behind them, aloof,
15 Shouldering the sky, patriarchal in serenity,
Blue Mountain Peak bulks.

And the professional gaze
Studies positions, impatiently waiting
For the perfect moment to fix
20 Their preparedness, to confine them
For the pleasant formality
Of the family album.

His brush a humming-bird
Meticulously poised . . .
25 The little hills fidgeting,
Changelessly changing,
Artlessly frustrating
The painter's art.

Vivian Virtue
b. JAMAICA 1911

Apologia

We the unknown, the abortive poets,
    Scribbling this and that, knowing
Full well the futility of all our efforts,
    Spoil for the critics' showing;
5 Knowing the impending dark wave
    Of oblivion in the offing which will shatter
Our souls' sandcastles, the wave which cries
    Halt to our rhymed chatter;
But knowing also that we must,
10   Must strive to pour
Out the heart's libation in thankfulness
    Though the wine be weak or sour;
For we, the unknown, the abortive poets,
    We too have clasped the rose
15 That flames upon the vision and dies soon,
    Too soon for the heart's repose.

Frank Collymore
b. BARBADOS 1893 d. 1980

For Harry Simmons

Brown, balding, with a lacertilian
jut to his underlip,
with spectacles thick as a glass paperweight
and squat, blunt fingers,
5 waspish, austere, swift with asperities,
with a dimpled pot for a belly from the red clay of Piaille.
Eyes like the glint of sea-smoothed bottle glass,
his knee-high khaki stockings,
brown shoes lacquered even in desolation.

10 People entered his understanding
like a wayside country church,
they had built him themselves.

It was they who had smoothed the wall
of his clay-coloured forehead,
15 who made of his rotundity an earthy
useful object
holding the clear water of their simple troubles,
he who returned their tribal names
to the adze, mattock, midden and cookingpot.

20 A tang of white rum on the tongue of the mandolin,
a young bay, parting its mouth,
a heron silently named or a night-moth,
or the names of villages plaited into one map,
in the evocation of scrubbed back-yard smoke,
25 and he is a man no more
but the fervour and intelligence
of a whole country.

Derek Walcott
b. ST. LUCIA 1930

Vocation

for Fr. Patrick Anthony

And so, despite the whisperings
behind hands clasped in fervent unbelief,
despite the stale, old lady's scent
of righteousness that crawls from
5   under French soutanes;
despite all that, and more

this is yours, you, your claim on love.

They could have asked. They could have asked
the blue smoked hills, the country mandolins;
10   old trembling-nosed, broad-voiced chantwelles
they could have asked; they could have asked tracks lost
but for some village's dying song;
        and belle-aire drums
        and violins
15   and moonlit ragged choirs,
        could have told and would have told
of what they'd always known:
that like a hidden mountain stream
caught patient swirling past the ages of the land
20   nothing dims that vision waiting gently:
        of calm clean pools below the waterfall.

And I
who share a common celibacy
that priests and poets must endure,
25   search that purity of syllable
seeking truths you've found;
incensed with love, I make too
that ritual of Word and Gesture,
wrists uplifted, fingers plucking
30   outward, scratching at this altar,
daring faith and hope, changing them
into some clarity.

John Robert Lee
b. CASTRIES, ST. LUCIA 1948

Mass Man

Through a great lion's head clouded by mange
a black clerk growls.
Next, a gold-wired peacock withholds a man,
a fan, flaunting its oval, jewelled eyes;
5   What metaphors!
What coruscating, mincing fantasies!

Hector Mannix, water-works clerk, San Juan, has entered a
lion,
Boysie, two golden mangoes bobbing for breastplates, barges
10   like Cleopatra down her river, making style.
'Join us,' they shout, 'O God, child, you can't dance?'
But somewhere in that whirlwind's radiance
a child, rigged like a bat, collapses, sobbing.

But I am dancing, look, from an old gibbet
15   my bull-whipped body swings, a metronome!
Like a fruit-bat dropped in the silk-cotton's shade,
my mania, my mania is a terrible calm.

Upon your penitential morning,
some skull must rub its memory with ashes,
20   some mind must squat down howling in your dust,
some hand must crawl and recollect your rubbish,
someone must write your poems.

Derek Walcott
b. ST. LUCIA 1930

Dilemmas

Corners Without Answers

They wonder when we spend
Hour after hour
Liming by corners, leaning on walls and lamp-posts
Sometimes silent, sometimes talking, or laughing hard
5 And always searching with shifty restless eyes.

On a hard road we struggle virgin bearded
Loud talking and brassed faced
Fighting to hold the fear within our hearts
The road beyond is misty blurred
10 The road behind we think was overrated.

They question when we sit
Night after night, on bar stools and in clubs
Twirling ice-filled glasses
Watching dark rum drop in bottles; steadily
15 Like barometers in bad weather.

In our ears the lips of old folk move
Telling of their golden generation; dignified, correct
But our skeptic thoughts refuse belief
Imperfect off-spring of perfection
20 Pseudo prophets not leaders and not led.

What if we run intent from love to love
If dark glasses hide the deceit mirrored in our eyes
What if we grimace long in grim pretence?
If we haunt ourselves with spectres of our own design.

25 At altar rails girls kneel expectant
We consecrate our love with fast shut eyes
Peeping to see the naked devil in their gaze
Beckoning to the ones that light our eyes

Through days and nights we form a crowd
30 Needing people near
And noise to shut out thoughts
Of how we are alone, all drifting souls.

We sit on pavements dreaming our dreams
Trying to invoke visions
35 No genie comes, disillusioned, we put bobs to buy
                                                another bottle
To help us endure this transition of sadness

Roger McTair
b. TRINIDAD 1943

Will the Real Me Please Stand Up?

As soon as i saw i was naked
i put on mother's dress
but it smelled of pain
and had holes where vanity had poked through

5 so i tried on father's coat
but it was too small for me
his ego being dwarfish

my brother's jacket
almost fit
10 but he had need of it

the circus was in town
a clown! that's it i thought, a clown!
but i didn't like the laughter, it got me down,

tin-hat, wig of judge, robe of priest,
15   i tried them all, for a while at least.

Animals seemed simply suited
so i concocted a beast to clothe in:
the elegant tights of a black panther
jerkin of a chameleon
20   and the hood of a Capuchin monkey

but the one i loved
said i was so beautiful
no one would undress me to go to bed with

something kinetic being needed
25   i appeared like a flock of white birds
circling over a green field

but the other i loved
said birds and fields were reminiscent of scarecrows
or Leda's bestialism
30   and was i sure i wasn't unsympathetic to homosexuals.

Therefore i decided to undress completely,
i unrolled my skin,
it came off neat as a banana,
carefully unstrapped my backbone and my guts,
35   stripped the pink flesh from the creamy bones
and threw them along with the bag of organs into the north wind
however secreting the sex-parts in my pocket,
not for utility
40   but because of their sculptured aesthetic,
the tactile and visual values, you understand.

Now i am carefully scanning
that relentless closed-circuit
which cameras and screens
45 every   thing
and when i pick me out
i will write again.

A. L. Hendriks
b. JAMAICA 1922

Theophilus Jones Walks Naked Down King Street

On Monday, October 18th,
Theophilus Jones took off
his asphalt-black, rag-tag pants
and walked naked down King Street.
5   It was a holiday –
and only a few people saw
his triumphant march,
his muscular, bearded-brown body,
his genitals flapping in front.
10 Theophilus Jones had wanted
to do this for a long time.

At Tower and King, three carwash boys
shouting 'Madman!', followed him to Harbour Street,
but seeing his indifference, turned
15 and dribbled back up the road.
Down on the Ferry Pier, a handful of people
waiting for the boat, stared out to sea
but did not see
Theophilus enter the water.

20   He walked out as far as possible,
     then began to swim, strongly and calmly,
     into the middle of the harbour.
     Eventually, way out in the deep,
     he stopped,
25   floated for a while, enjoying the sun,
     watched a plane take off from the green-rimmed palisades,
     and then, letting himself go,
     allowed the water
     to swallow him up.

30   Theophilus Jones went down
     slowly,
     slowly his bent legs, slowly
     his arms above his head,
     slowly his locksed hair,
35   slowly.
     Until nothing could be seen of him.
     Some orange peel, an old tin-can
     and a sea-saturated cigarette box
     floated over his demise,
40   while nearby,
     a kingfisher – scavenging for sprats
     on a low current – veered down
     and landed,
     in a spray of sunlit water.

                                         Heather Royes
                                         b. JAMAICA

Choice of Corpses

suppose you found a man
a little from now
the next few minutes
hiding in your room:
5   a revolutionary
but with no sanction
from a revolutionary government
not yet gloriously dead
    like Che
10 and not triumphantly alive
    like Fidel

just a man in sweaty khaki
smelling a little of bush
and metal, and madness

15 suppose you found a man
    in your room
    thirsty with fear
    his eyes bright with hunger
    his vision at a temperature
20   of 400 years
    what would you say?
      Venceremos?

suppose he didn't speak Spanish?
    Or Russian?
25   Or Chinese?
but some type of
Afro-Caribbean English?
Would that be alright?
I mean, you wouldn't
30 get suspicious?

suppose you found a man
a little from now,
a revolutionary
inside your head
35 behind your closed eyelids
crouching below your tongue
   and he said
    to let him out
or he would rot inside you

40 suppose you had
a choice of corpses?

Kendel Hippolyte
b. JAMAICA 1952

Portia Faces Life

E don' ave no car, e don' ave no bike,
to work e hitch-hike

all de while
Portia saying
5 **she facing life.**

Pon top e head
de sun tearing a bite
madmen and acrobats performing at the traffic lights

all de while
10 Portia saying how
she facing life.

Where Lodge begin at Durban and Vlissengen
stands a lady on the corner with a bucket o' newspaper
by the bridge that cars play jump-in
15 on a road which lead where the dead livin

all de while
Portia saying
is life she facing.

Marbles going to school
20   roll in the gutter in front of two little boys
like traffic lights playing follow de leader

all de while
Portia saying
is life she facing.

25   And de sun don' shine
is just gettin hotter
like a sign-post insisting Drink rum not water

leaning on a drunk bus-stop one century after the disaster
Portia still saying
30   **'What's the matter**
though I'm getting older, I can't feel better
Aunt Mary's left the Palms with the doctor
for the local cinema to perform Shakespeare's
                              "Aha-lah-wallah-wallah".'

Like Scott Fitzgerald, only blacker,
35   he stands by the bar with some cat call Soldier
singing calypso wid Solomon and Pharoah
getting drunk on rum and water

an de Guyana radio station at half-mast
broadcast a memoriam to some jumbee general
40   called Eisenhower

then came an announcement
that Santa will soon be here to do the samba
like Rock-a-fellah.

Jus den
45 **Portia faces life**

an a truck turn over
in de gutter flows a coco-cola river
an a litter of birds fall from a tree
like nutten is de matter.

Marc Matthews
b. GUYANA 1937

Noah

for Mervyn Morris

Everywhere fish wheeled and fled
Or died in scores, floating like eggs.
From his mind's ark, Noah,
Sailor for the kingdom of Truth's sake,
5 Watched the water close like mouths
Over the last known hills. Next day
He slept, dreaming of haystacks.

Water woke him. He stood, arms folded,
Looking out of a porthole, thinking nothing,
10 Numbed to a stare by horizon's drone, and the
Dry patter of rain. On the third day,
Decisive, sudden, he dragged
Down the canvas curtain and turned
Inward to tend his animals, his
15 Animals, waking with novelty.

Locked, driven by fatigue, the ark
Beat and beat across the same sea,
Bloated, adrift, finding
Nothing to fasten to.
20 Barnacles grew up the side like sores. Inside,

Noah, claustrophobic, sat and watched
The occupants of his ark take on
New aspects, shudder into focus, one
By one. Something, he thought, must come
25   Of this. Such isolation! Such concentration!
Out of these instinctual, half-lit lives,
Something: some good, some Truth!
That night a dropped calf bawled to its feet,
Shaking off light like dirt.

30   Noah, an old man, unhappy, shook
His head. Birth was not the answer,
Nor death: his mind's ark stank
Of birth and death, would always,
Sundering, stink. Outside,
35   The hard insistent patter of rain
Saying 'Think, Noah think! Break this
Patter of rain, man!' But only animals
Moved in his mind.
                              Now, unbodied by raindrops,
The patter continued, empty, shelled,
40   Clambering down along itself like crabs.
Driven, impotent, he neared despair.

Finally one bird, unasked, detached itself
And battered around inside his skull.
Thankfully Noah released it, fearful,
45   Hoping, watching it flit and bang
Against wind, returning each time
Barren. Till one day, laden with lies,
It brought back promise of fruit, of
Resolution and change.

50   Now animals and men crowded the gangplank,
Peering eagerly about the returning hills
For some sign of change. Noah conducted them,
Drifting among valleys with breaking smiles,
Naming, explaining, directing: Noah, released,
55   Turned once more outwards, giving thanks.

Relief dazed them: nobody realized
Nothing had changed. Animal and man
Settled quietly to old moulds, un-
Remembered seasons of death and birth,
60 Led by the bearded one, the prophet, Noah
Rejuvenated, giving thanks on a hill,
Moving among known animals and men
With a new aspect, giving thanks . . . While,

Leaking, derelict, its mission abandoned,
65 The ark of his mind
Wallowed empty westward
To where all rainbows
Drown among waves

Wayne Brown
b. TRINIDAD 1944

Adios, Carenage

In idle August, while the sea soft,
and leaves of brown islands stick to the rim
of this Caribbean, I blow out the light
by the dreamless face of Maria Concepcion
5 to ship as a seaman on the schooner *Flight*.
Out in the yard turning gray in the dawn,
I stood like a stone and nothing else move
but the cold sea rippling like galvanize
and the nail holes of stars in the sky roof,
10 till a wind start to interfere with the trees.
I pass me dry neighbor sweeping she yard
as I went downhill, and I nearly said:
'Sweep soft, you witch, 'cause she don't sleep hard,'
but the bitch look through me like I was dead.

15 A route taxi pull up, park-lights still on.
The driver size up my bags with a grin:
'This time, Shabine, like you really gone!'
I ain't answer the ass, I simple pile in
the back seat and watch the sky burn
20 above Laventille pink as the gown
in which the woman I left was sleeping,
and I look in the rearview and see a man
exactly like me, and the man was weeping
for the houses, the streets, that whole stinking island.

25 Christ have mercy on all sleeping things!
From that dog rotting down Wrightson Road
to when I was a dog on these streets;
if loving these islands must be my load,
out of corruption my soul takes wings.
30 But they had started to poison my soul
with their big house, big car, big-time bohbohl,
coolie, nigger, Syrian, and French Creole,
so I leave it for them and their carnival –
I taking a sea bath, I gone down the road.
35 I know these islands from Monos to Nassau,
a rusty head sailor with sea-green eyes
that they nickname Shabine, the patois for
any red nigger, and I, Shabine, saw
when these slums of empire was paradise.
40 I'm just a red nigger who love the sea,
I had a sound colonial education,
I have Dutch, nigger, and English in me,
and either I'm nobody, or I'm a nation.

But Maria Concepcion was all my thought
45 watching the sea heaving up and down
as the port side of dories, schooners, and yachts
was painted afresh by the strokes of the sun
signing her name with every reflection;
I knew when dark-haired evening put on
50 her bright silk at sunset, and, folding the sea,
sidled under the sheet with her starry laugh,
that there'd be no rest, there'd be no forgetting.

Is like telling mourners round the graveside
about resurrection, they want the dead back,
55 so I smile to myself as the bow rope untied
and the *Flight* swing seaward: 'Is no use repeating
that the sea have more fish. I ain't want her
dressed in the sexless light of a seraph,
I want those round brown eyes like a marmoset, and
60 till the day when I can lean back and laugh,
those claws that tickled my back on sweating
Sunday afternoons, like a crab on wet sand.'
As I worked, watching the rotting waves come
past the bow that scissor the sea like silk,
65 I swear to you all, by my mother's milk,
by the stars that shall fly from tonight's furnace,
that I loved them, my children, my wife, my home;
I loved them as poets love the poetry
that kills them, as drowned sailors the sea.

70 You ever look up from some lonely beach
and see a far schooner? Well, when I write
this poem, each phrase go be soaked in salt;
I go draw and knot every line as tight
as ropes in this rigging; in simple speech
75 my common language go be the wind,
my pages the sails of the schooner *Flight*.
But let me tell you how this business begin.

Derek Walcott
b. ST. LUCIA 1930

Time, Folkways, Religion

Ol' Higue

Ol' woman wid de wrinkled skin,
Leh de ol' higue wuk begin.
Put on you fiery disguise,
Ol' woman wid de weary eyes.
5   Shed you swizzly skin.

Ball o' fire, raise up high.
Raise up till you touch de sky.
Land 'pon top somebody roof.
Tri'pse in through de keyhole—poof!
10   -   Open you ol' higue eye.

Find de baby where 'e lie.
Change back faster than de eye.
Find de baby, lif' de sheet,
Mek de puncture wid you teet',
15   Suck de baby dry.

Before 'e wake an' start to cry,
Change back fast, an' out you fly.
Find de goobie wid you skin.
Mek you semidodge, then – in!
20   Grin you ol' higue grin.

In your dutty-powder gown
Next day schoolchildren flock you round.
"Ol' higue, ol' higue!" dey hollerin' out.
Tek it easy, hold you mout'.
25   Doan leh dem find you out.

Dey gwine mark up wid a chalk
Everywhere wheh you got to walk –
You bridge, you door, you jalousie –
But cross de marks an' leh dem see.
30   Else dey might spread de talk.

Next night you gone out jus' de same,
Wrap up in you ball o'flame,
To find an' suck another child.
But tikkay! Rumour spreadin' wild.
35   An' people know you name.

Fly across dis window-sill.
Why dis baby lyin' so still?
Lif' de sheet like how you does do.
Oh God! Dis baby nightgown blue!
40   Run fo' de window-sill!

Woman you gwine run or not?
Doan mind de rice near to de cot.
De smell o' asafoetida
Like um tek effect 'pon you.
45   You wan' get kyetch or what?

But now is too late for advice,
'Cause you done start to count de rice
An' if you only drop one grain
You must begin it all again.
50   But you gwine count in vain.

Whuh ah tell you?

Day done light an' rice still mountin'
Till dey wake an' kyetch you countin'
An' pick up de big fat cabbage broom
55 An' beat you all around de room.
          Is now you should start countin'

Whaxen! Whaxen! Whaxen! Plai!
You gwine pay fo' you sins befo' you die.
Lash she all across she head.
60 You suck me me baby till um dead?
          Whaxen! Whaxen! Plai!

You feel de manicole 'cross you hip?
Beat she till blood start to drip.
"Ow me God! You bruk me hip!
65 Done now, nuh? Allyou done!"

Is whuh you sayin' deh, you witch?
Done? Look, allyou beat de bitch.
Whaxen! Whaxen! Pladai! Plai!
Die, you witch you. Die!
70 Whaxen!
          Whaxen!
                    Plai!

Wordsworth A. McAndrew
b. GUYANA 1928

Sister Mary and the Devil

I was going down the road
and the two O'clock sun
only beating down on the
roses on Brother Williams wreath
5 till them curl up like them want to
sleep,
and is only me and God
alone
Going down the road.

10 the dust was powdering
mi clean white shoes
when I look down
and see mi shadow double.

I know him was the devil.
15 him never have to tell mi
because mi blood start to run
and stop
and heavy down mi step
and the ground leave
20 mi foot
and mi heart like it want
stop
and I wash wid cold sweat.

The devil himself
25 a tall man in full black
with a hat that cover him
face like a umbrella.
then him take brother Williams
wreath from me
30 and him hold mi round mi waist

and fire catch in mi body
and I shame and hide mi face
and then him talk for the first
time
35 and it was there
Sister Mary died
when the devil
in him
satan voice
40 hold on to
the wreath and Said
today is Mine Sister Mary
let the dead
Bury the dead.

Lorna Goodison
b. JAMAICA 1947

Tabiz

Long time ago they used to say
How jumbie used to walk the road

this poem is to cut maljo
is to save you from the blight
of overloving eyes that conceal hate
from over-generous eyes that subsume
5   the bitter bile of envy
from judas-friendly eyes that shut
bestowing the betraying kiss

like a blue bottle on a stick
it will ward off whatsoever evil
10   may try to wither the bounty
of your blooming life's garden

keep it there and no beetle
no bug no worm no fly no snake
will invade and your life
15   will be a blossoming eden

then you'll sing your happy songs
in the peaceful harmony you wish
and all your joys will be unsullied

or wear it like a mystic amulet
20   or a ringlet of blue-black beads
or yet like a blessed ankh
and feel your confidence rise
as you scale the unsurmountable
wear it and you'll climb your everests
25   as easily as your el tucuches

or make of it a magic circle
to protect and comfort you
step into it as my friend's mother once
IN HOC VINCIT and with signs
30 defied her enemies
and the evil ones
we'll chant the aves halleluias
the hosannas the alaikums and oms
we'll bring the greater glory
35 to your assistance and you will
rise and soar

or make it a stole of blue
draping your possessed shoulders
making all your ancestral contacts
40 give you great strength

encircled by the indigoed words
you will bravely step through
legs of phantoms
put salt on soucouyant skins
45 make doens disappear
and you'll dance in life's moonlight
safe from all harm

Anson Gonzales
b. TRINIDAD 1934

Guard-ring

Moon shadow burning,
Watch where I walking, Lord.
Make mi foot step hard
on the enemy's shadow
5 an hear me.

I wearing de ring dem tonight –
one gainst hate and de red pepper
tongue of malice, a snake-eye
bone-ring to touch
10 if I buck up de tempter,
one ring gainst love-me
an one gainst de finger of famine,
an one for the death by drowning,
an one from fire;
15 an a bright copper ring
that I fine in a fish belly,
tun me safe an salt
from de barracuta teet of desire.

But moon shadow falling.
20 I fraid for de shape of de winding –
de road too crooked,
it making a rope to twine me!
An Lord, I tired
to tell yu mi torment, but listen
25 an learn me, an reach me
to home. I believe
in de blessed ring, but Chris'
I praising yu candle also,
I raising mi heart like a smalls,
30 like a coal that outing
to light it –
                    guard me asleep an awake!
De ring did bless in de balm yard
but Thee I praise.
35 I singing out loud
for de hill dem to hear me an tremble

Dennis Scott
b. JAMAICA 1939

Uncle Time

Uncle Time is a ole, ole man . . .
All year long 'im wash 'im foot in de sea
long, lazy years on de wet san'
an shake de coconut tree dem
5   quiet-like wid 'im sea-win laughter,
scraping away de lan' . . .

Uncle Time is a spider-man, cunnin' an cool,
him tell you: watch de hill an yu si me.
Huhh! Fe yu yi no quick enough fe si
10   how 'im move like mongoose; man, yu tink 'im fool?

Me Uncle Time smile black as sorrow;
'im voice is sof' as bamboo leaf
but Lawd, me Uncle cruel.
When 'im play in de street
15   wid yu woman, – watch 'im! By tomorrow
she dry as cane-fire, bitter as cassava;
an when 'im teach yu son, long after
yu walk wid stranger, an yu bread is grief.
Watch how 'im spin web roun yu house, an creep
20   inside; an when 'im touch yu, weep . . .

Dennis Scott
b. JAMAICA 1939

So Long, Charlie Parker

The night before he died
the bird walked on and played

his heart out: notes fell
like figure-forming pebbles

5   in a pond. he
     was angry: and we

     knew he wept to know his time had come
     so soon. so little had been done

     so little time to do it in

10   he wished to hold the night from burning
     all time long. but time

     is short
     and life
     is short
15   and breath
     is short

     and so he
     slowed and
     slurred and
20   stopped. his
     fingers fixed
     upon a minor key:
     then slipped

     his bright eyes blazed and bulged against the death in him then
25   knocking at the door

     he watched:
     as one will watch a great clock striking time from a great booming
         midnight bell:
     the silence slowly throbbing in behind the dying bell

30   the night before he died
     the bird walked on through fear through faith through frenzy that
         he tried
     to hide but could not stop that bell

                                            Edward Brathwaite
                                            b. BARBADOS 1930

for Don Cosmic
Don

'To John Coltrane: the heaviest spirit'
Inscription *Black Music*, LeRoi Jones/Imamu Baraka

may I learn the shape of that hurt
which captured you nightly into
dread city, discovering through
streets steep with the sufferer's beat;

5   Teach me to walk through jukeboxes
& shadow that broken music
whose irradiant stop is light,
guide through those mournfullest journeys

I back into harbour Spirit
10 in heavens remember we now
& show we a way in to praise,
all seekers to-gather, one-heart:

and let we lock conscious when wrong
& Babylon rock back again:
15 in the evil season sustain
o heaviest spirit of sound.

Anthony McNeill
b. JAMAICA 1941

The Tree

Leave me to my little land
Tethered like a tree,
Near the loves I understand –
Loves that nurture me.

5   Let my roots go deep, go deep,
Seeking fabled streams
While the trade winds sound and sweep
Through my leafy dreams

Let the fierce wide noontide heat
10   Haunt my sap with pain;
Afterwards will seem more sweet
Revelry of rain,

And the stir of all wild things,
Hares, and bees, and birds,
15   Turn my faint imaginings
Into golden words.

Then above the day's vain noise,
Strong, secure, at peace,
I shall spread essential joys
20   For the world's release,

Save that, in the light or dark
When two lovers come,
I shall tremble as I hark,
Tranced like them and dumb.

H. A. Vaughan
b. SANTO DOMINGO 1901

There Runs a Dream

There runs a dream of perished Dutch plantations
In these Guiana rivers to the sea.
Black waters, rustling through the vegetation
That towers and tangles banks, run silently
5 Over lost stellings where the craft once rode
Easy before trim dwellings in the sun
And fields of indigo would float out broad
To lose the eye right on the horizon.

These rivers know that strong and quiet men
10 Drove back a jungle, gave Guiana root
Against the shock of circumstance, and then
History moved down river, leaving free
The forest to creep back, foot by quiet foot,
And overhang black waters to the sea.

A. J. Seymour
b. GUYANA 1914

PART TWO

This Land

Holy

Holy be the white head of a Negro.
Sacred be the black flax of a black child.
Holy be
The golden down
5   That will stream in the waves of the winds
And will thin like dispersing cloud.
Holy be
Heads of Chinese hair
Sea calm, sea impersonal,
10   Deep flowering of the mellow and traditional.
Heads of peoples fair
Bright, shimmering from the riches of their species;
Heads of Indians
With feelings of distance and space and dusk:
15   Heads of wheaten gold,
Heads of peoples dark
So strong, so original:
All of the earth and the sun!

George Campbell
b. JAMAICA 1918

This Land

Under this rhythm
Beats the voice
No one will notice.

Under this rock
5   Is the flame
No one sends freedom.

Under this island
Is the land
No one desires.

10 But in the time of drought
Is weeping
And in the time of harvest
Is weeping
And at the funeral
15 Is weeping
And in the marriage-bed
Is weeping.

Look O my Sun
Over this island
20 Look O my stars
Into this island.

For it sits upon the doorstep
And waits
And there is bleating in the dawn
25 And there is bleating in the night
For it sits upon the doorstep
And waits.

land has no centre
ther direction.
ere is smoke without fire.
ife without movement.
      This! Oh my land.

                    M. G. Smith
                    b. JAMAICA 1921

The Village

I know this village. I was born and bred here;
Grew up in that shanty there across the road;
Went to that little shop for groceries:
For things like flour, rice, salt-fish and pork;
5 And took my turn there at the village pipe.

This village is a part of me: I know no other.
Each little home, each jaunty little hut
Is just another part of me. These wooden homes
That look so bravely to the rising sun, are limbs –
10 My limbs. I watched them sprout through toil and agony.

For once this spot was all the world I knew:
It nourished me with wisdom from its breast.
As knowledge spiralled like an airy web,
This spot remained the hub and centre of my life,
15 And coloured all the texture of my dreams.

This village, too, has grown, but slow, so slow!
It seems to hang in space like yonder old mile-tree.
It has not learned to speak the language of the town,
Much to the sorrow of my friends. Ah no!
20 Its wisdom broods above the festooned cane.

Maybe, I'll roam to cities far and wide,
And learn to speak, some day, the language of the towns:
But here remains the one romantic spot
That has its roots deep, deep within my soul,
25   This and my mother, deep primeval ties.

William S. Arthur
b. BARBADOS 1909

The Village

Moonlight and lonely ways,
A strolling pair;
Restless, the canefields lisp
And murmur fear.

5   Grass bordered paths that wind
Mystic and white,
Into far fairyland
Eluding sight.

Close huddled rustic shacks
10   Like frightened sheep;
Grim jaws of yawning hills
And valleys deep;

Age-gray, the village Church
Guarding its dead,
15   Upon whose grassy mounds
Moonbeams are spread.

Karl Sealy
b. BARBADOS 1932

To Those

To those
Who lifted into shape
The huge stones of the pyramid;
Who formed the Sphinx in the desert,
5 And bid it
Look down upon the centuries like yesterday;
Who walked lithely
On the banks of the Congo,
And heard the deep rolling moan
10 Of the Niger;
And morning and evening
Hit the brave trail of the forest
With the lion and the elephant;
To those
15 Who, when it came that they should leave
Their urns of history behind,
Left only with a sad song in their hearts;
And burst forth into soulful singing
As bloody pains of toil
20 Strained like a hawser at their hearts
To those, hail . . .

Harold Telemaque
b. TOBAGO 1909

Ancestor on the Auction Block

Ancestor on the auction block
Across the years your eyes seek mine
Compelling me to look.
I see your shackled feet
5 Your primitive black face
I see your humiliation
And turn away
Ashamed.

Across the years your eyes seek mine
10 Compelling me to look
Is this mean creature that I see
Myself?
Ashamed to look
Because of myself ashamed
15 Shackled by my own ignorance
I stand
A slave.

Humiliated
I cry to the eternal abyss
20 For understanding
Ancestor on the auction block
Across the years your eyes meet mine
Electric
I am transformed
25 My freedom is within myself.

I look you in the eyes and see
The spirit of God eternal
Of this only need I be ashamed
Of blindness to the God within me
30 The same God who dwelt within you
The same eternal God
Who shall dwell
In generations yet unborn.

Ancestor on the auction block
35 Across the years
I look
I see you sweating, toiling, suffering
Within your loins I see the seed
Of multitudes
40 From your labour
Grow roads, aqueducts, cultivation
A new country is born
Yours was the task to clear the ground
Mine be the task to build.

Vera Bell
b. JAMAICA 1906

For Christopher Columbus

At night Columbus paced the poop alone.
Hard to hold men to a vision.
                              The faith fails
Sometimes even in the dreamer.

5   Signs, signs.
Today a little branch full of dogroses
Drifted along the ocean's breathing bosom
Imagine roses in ocean
Roses at the edge of the world

10 The sea was calm like the river of Seville
A day ago and breeze as soft as April
Made fragrant wing to our weary caravels.

Vision, yes, vision.
                        I, an Italian
15 Holding three Spanish crews to an unknown land
After how many desert years.
A young man, poor, dreaming on Ptolemy
With his globe, and the maps of Marinus of Tyre,
And the opinion of Alfraganus the Arabian
20 That the world is not as large as people think

And living in the pages of Marco Polo
The Venetian feted once by the Great Khan.

Sometimes dreams harden and blaze into a vision
That leads the man to hostile courts and wars.

25 Fighting against the Moors – but the vision blazing
In the warrior's head.

> Answering bald-headed friars
Within the Salamanca Council Room.
What St. Augustine and the sages said
30 How Adam's sons never had crossed the ocean
And peopled the antipodes – answering friars
With the vision burning.

Man must endure the crumbling powers, the crack
Of another's will but hold his vision fast,
35 Whip muscle and nerve to keep appointed pace
Drive wheel for westward to the couching sun.

Man must adventure to the Sun's declension
Translate his vision into a tower of fact
Despite the loosening limbs, the unstable powers
40 Failing about him.

Vision moulds clay into a hero despite the man
Cuts him to the brains and drives him hungry
To bring an inviolate star down to the earth.
Vision may break a man to make a city,

45 Vision's an edge to civilisation, carving
Beauty from wilderness and charting seas.
Visionless, man falls back into the animal
With Nature striding in her ancient places.

And look, look – look, a light, – Quick, Pedro,
50 come.

A. J. Seymour
b. GUYANA 1914

The Age of Chains

from Patterns, A Caribbean Sequence

Isn't history amazing?
One time it is gold, or a basket of fish;
Another time it is a woman.
Sometimes it is oil, or perhaps a disagreement
5   With a Pope.
But mostly it is a stranger on the road to Emmaus.
We recognise it gone.

(God winks for a brief century and a world rots.
One man asked for three days more
10   And found my world).

Beautiful was my country in time's rains.
Beautiful is my country in the warm hopeful season.
An age of chains did not sully her mountains,
Nor pain's broad knuckle smudge out the sun.
15   O Beautiful.

I catch her voice in the thick-haired hills,
her impulse. Gathers green in the wood
her breath skying. In the quick tempo of the river
I hear her high singing. A song that is good.
20   O beautiful.

Up and far beyond care of the wind's corroding,
ruin of star and light's utter end,
toil and her heart's hopes extend
beautiful.
25   Sun's her monument;
and her brightness is of a bright sky's hoarding.

If you see Zaccheus or Balboa
They will define you destiny from a tree.
Drowsing on a cloud I see
30   A ship bulging westward, with a cargo of groans below . . .

Commandante Nicolas de Ovando
Enjoyed being Governor of San' Domingo.
All the Indians worshipped Nicolas
All men admired Nicolas
35 Except perhaps the priest las Casas
Bartoleme de las Casas, *Apostol de las Indias*.
The priest did not like the way Ovando was killing out
the Indians in the cane fields.
Nicolas did not much mind, but he respected priests.

40 Nicolas did not mean to be cruel
But Spain must be strong, and in any case
You could not leave cane standing in the field forever.
(They say the hurricane waits for the time of ripe cane.)
    So when the ships began arriving,
45 And the big black beasts were walked up and down the decks.
Ovando bought the first boatload for the field.
For this all men admired Nicolas,
Even the priest de las Casas, *Apostol de las Indias*.
The new beasts hated Nicolas with a strong black hate.

50 (O, Hawkins was a sturdy fellow.
White were his teeth as the teeth of the raven.
They buried him in the sea off Puerto Rico).
As near heaven . . .

Drowsing on a cloud I watch islands
55 Soon swarming with black labour.
Life is hot sun and a hot whip
And a more than casual acquaintance with dust.
The old and lucky graduate from
Mud to the master's table
60 The Big Place.
Some of the masters come down to the warmth
Where the plump girls wait to proffer
Out of fear their dumb efficient embrace.
Africa is lost,
65 (Hills, O strange woman)
And only a broken syllable records her speech;

(Afrika godzi miya ba)
Only a granite rhythm redeems her music;
(O flirter with time)
70 Only in a private whisper, her soul.
Labour now is without dignity
But the nobility of flesh is not perished.
For in these fields though the slave's
Blood snap and the master weaken his own soul,
75 Both in the end are martyrs, and bear chains,
The crop's the tyrant. Sugar is king.
And only whip of the ripe cane's blade is soulless.

Africa is not lost.
My fathers sing the sun in one remembered syllable,
80 And freedom is preserved in private whispers.

E. McG. Keane
b. ST. VINCENT 1927

Islands

Islands are droppings
of mud and rock;
selfcentred, selfsatisfied;
should sink forever.

5 Who will care?

Droppings
of love.
Islands are screams
solidified, washed with passion.

10 Islands are mystical spaces
cursed with history, gripped, blinded
by illusions; peopled with madmen,
jokers, dreamers.

Islands are poems
15 totally useless, except
to those who use them, have use
for them;
those who care

Islands: poems to people
20 Some care.

Roger McTair
b. TRINIDAD 1943

Like Music Suddenly

Near the last corner of this small seaport
an old ochre building
has waded into low water
and stands passively watching the blue bay.

5 the walls of this house are dry and wrinkled
with deciduous paint;
two green faded shutters
(occasionally moved by lazy hands)
seem like reflective eyes studying the horizon;

10 on the shore there are girls
whose sea-bright splashed limbs shine
and flash dark radiance:
                                        they are laughing
and that sharp sound knocks
and rebounds off those old house-walls.

15 Because there are moored boats; because
this small sea-village hangs its rust-coloured
gossamer fishing-nets towards the sun;
(frail spiderwebs across tree branches!);
because a yellow building blinks
20 slow compassionate eyes
at a horizon few men know,
these wet girls floating loud gaiety upon the bay
are like music suddenly.

A. L. Hendriks
b. JAMAICA 1922

Hex

I

So she sings of streams
that are a-glutter with boulders

of rocks that have not forgotten
their ancestry of iron

5   she quarrels like the dry seeds of the lotus rattle

she rattles like dry tamarind pods
like shak shaks

she shakes
and her tongue climbs a hill of dry consonants

10   she is alpha
she is omega
she is happy

it is not failure that disturbs her:
she dreams and interprets her dreams

15   it is not crack of faith that disturbs her
she has seen too many ghosts

it is not fear:
for she is always alone

II

but she weepeth long into the night
20   white trail of salt is there upon her cheek
among her loves, there is none left to comfort her
all her friends, ladies of fashion
parsons of bibles of temper, beggars who hurled stones
into the mangrove stores
25   all have dealt treacherously with her

her feet know quicksand
her steps know the slough of despond
the pathways, the doors, the jealousy windows,

outlooks of uncertain knowledge:
30 eyes peep glint steel:
these are now certainly enemies
and because her inheritance is swallowed by strangers:
her houses, her beaches, the views of her landscape
from which the youngsters sap milk
35 are turned over to tourists: to terrorists:
she mothers us as if we were orphans and fatherless
as if she were a witch or a widow of prophets.
all the peaks, the promontories, the coves, the glitter.

bays of her body have been turned into money
40 the grass ploughed up and fed into mortar of houses
for master for mister for massa for mortal baas
her sands are now owned by the minister midas
and have been burned into careful gold brochures
the leaves of her trees are now printed in amsterdam
45 her breadfruit is sold into foreigner factories
and returned to her sons wrapped up in tins to be eaten as chips
and the lips of the bankers smile as they rip her children to debts
there is more weed than food in the island

Edward Brathwaite
b. BARBADOS 1930

After the Storm

There's a fresh light that follows a storm
while the whole sea still havoc; in its bright wake
I saw the veiled face of Maria Concepcion
marrying the ocean, then drifting away
5   in the widening lace of her bridal train
with white gulls her bridesmaids, till she was gone.
I wanted nothing after that day.
Across my own face, like the face of the sun,
a light rain was falling, with the sea calm.

10   Fall gently, rain, on the sea's upturned face
like a girl showering; make these islands fresh
as Shabine once knew them! Let every trace,
every hot road, smell like clothes she just press
and sprinkle with drizzle. I finish dream;
15   whatever the rain wash and the sun iron:
the white clouds, the sea and sky with one seam,
is clothes enough for my nakedness.
Though my *Flight* never pass the incoming tide
of this inland sea beyond the loud reefs
20   of the final Bahamas, I am satisfied
if my hand gave voice to one people's grief.
Open the map. More islands there, man,
than peas on a tin plate, all different size,
one thousand in the Bahamas alone,
25   from mountains to low scrub with coral keys,
and from this bowsprit, I bless every town,
the blue smell of smoke in hills behind them,
and the one small road winding down them like twine
to the roofs below; I have only one theme:

30   The bowsprit, the arrow, the longing, the lunging heart –
the flight to a target whose aim we'll never know,
vain search for one island that heals with its harbour
and a guiltless horizon, where the almond's shadow
doesn't injure the sand. There are so many islands!
35   As many islands as the stars at night
on that branched tree from which meteors are shaken
like falling fruit around the schooner *Flight*.

But things must fall, and so it always was,
on one hand Venus, on the other Mars;
40 fall, and are one, just as this earth is one
island in archipelagoes of stars.
My first friend was the sea. Now, is my last.
I stop talking now. I work, then I read,
cotching under a lantern hooked to the mast.
45 I try to forget what happiness was,
and when that don't work, I study the stars.
Sometimes is just me, and the soft-scissored foam
as the deck turn white and the moon open
a cloud like a door, and the light over me
50 is a road in white moonlight taking me home.
Shabine sang to you from the depths of the sea.

Derek Walcott
b. ST. LUCIA 1930

I Shall Return

I shall return again, I shall return
To laugh and love and watch with wonder-eyes
At golden noon the forest fires burn,
Wafting their blue-black smoke to sapphire skies.
5 I shall return to loiter by the streams
That bathe the brown blades of the bending grasses,
And realize once more my thousand dreams
Of waters surging down the mountain passes.
I shall return to hear the fiddle and fife
10 Of village dances, dear delicious tunes
That stir the hidden depths of native life,
Stray melodies of dim-remembered runes.
I shall return. I shall return again
To ease my mind of long, long years of pain.

Claude McKay
b. JAMAICA 1889 d. 1948

Residue

I
The wind is crisp and carries
a tang of the sea. The flowers
burn richly against the grass.
The grass itself shines and is
precious.

II
5 Ahead, the sky and the ocean
merge in a stain of blue. On the beach
yesterday, lolloping tourists
were posting umbrellas like crosses.

III
This morning I chose to stay home,
10 To watch the cats and think of
Columbus. And the grass is precious
merely because it belongs to us.

Anthony McNeill
b. JAMAICA 1941

Struggle and Endurance

The Riders

Over the hill in the mist of the morning
I see them a-coming, an army a-wheel:
Four abreast, six abreast, the road keeps on spawning
Them, hard-riding men with faces of steel.

5 Young men and old men, they ride on together,
None paying heed to the one at his side;
Toe to toe; wheel to wheel; crouched on the leather
Seats, over their handle-bars, onward they ride.

Grim must their faces be; theirs is the ride of life,
10 Bread's at the end of it, and leisure to follow;
Bread for a mother or sister or wife,
A toy for the kid or a kiss in the Hollow.

Out of the distance and into the view they come,
Hundreds of men with their feet on the pedals;
15 The sweat on their faces, hear how their cycles hum,
Riding for bread, not for glory or medals.

Barnabas J. Ramon-Fortuné
b. TRINIDAD 1917

All Men Come to the Hills

All men come to the hills
Finally ....

Men from the deeps of the plains of the sea –
Where a wind-in-the-sail is hope,
5   That long desire, and long weariness fulfils –
Come again to the hills.

And men with dusty, broken feet;
Proud men, lone men like me,
Seeking again the soul's deeps –
10   Or a shallow grave
Far from the tumult of the wave –
Where a bird's note motions the silence in ....
The white kiss of silence that the spirit stills
Still as a cloud of windless sail horizon-hung
15   above the blue glass of the sea –
Come again to the hills ....

Come ever, finally.

Roger Mais
b. JAMAICA 1905 d. 1955

Death of a Comrade

Death must not find us thinking that we die.

Too soon, too soon
our banner draped for you.
I would prefer
5   the banner in the wind
not bound so tightly
in a scarlet fold —
not sodden sodden
with your people's tears
10   but flashing on the pole
we bear aloft
down and beyond this dark dark lane of rags.

Dear Comrade
if it must be
15   you speak no more with me
nor smile no more with me
then let me take
a patience and a calm –
for even now the greener leaf explodes
20   sun brightens stone
and all the river burns.

Now from the mourning vanguard moving on
dear Comrade I salute you and I say
Death will not find us thinking that we die.

Martin Carter
b. GUYANA 1927

from **Rain Mosaic**

Narrator: There was a time the sky was indigo.
          The clouds stiff and staring, the earth
          Bone dry and no rain came. The face of the fields
          Had fallen and the canes died on their feet. The
5   colour
          Of rust ran among the green and the green was
          snuffed
          A shiver was the hard soil and the air spelt earth
          quake.
10   Hunger became a silly companion, a customary
          hanger-on
          And men's eyes grew tired with the strain of watch-
          ing.

1st Voice: And men's hearts matched the hardness of the sky.

15 *2nd Voice*:   And hatred served their hunger

1st Voice: They burnt the canes in the day and the aches flew
          Black and high like insects along the dull streets
          Or fell to earth like hopes dehydrated.

2nd Voice: They burnt the canes at night and in the night sky
20   The burning light was a fresco stained by a demon
          hand.

1st Voice: And the ribs of the earth were naked

2nd Voice: The soil like a twisted rind refused to flower

1st Voice: Refused the blossom and the seed ...

25 *Narrator*:   The moonlight was a liar and a cheat, flinging
          Its net to gather foolish hopes. The boys and girls
          Shouted their bright games while the old
          Sat and mused
          Or made a commonwealth of sorrow. The moonlight

30 *1st Voice*: Was fresh as a vegetable new upon a stem

2nd Voice: Distilled like love-drops
From the laboratory of the eyes.

1st Voice: A pool of delight for children and lovers

35 *Narrator*: But for men unstarred the moon was an alien
A satellite of another country and there was anguish
In the heart.

2nd Voice: And one stark evening beneath the street lamp

1st Voice: While men grumbled over their sick gambling

2nd Voice: Thin-winged flies appeared and held session
Over their heads

40 *1st Voice*: And the air was chill and lonely
Upon the cheek

2nd Voice: And the wind stood up and sped wildly
About the prairies of the sky

1st Voice: And men stared

45 *Narrator*: And the rain came at last, suddenly, voluminously.
It came in cascades down the slopes of heaven.
It tumbled like tomes from the shelves of the sky.
It rode the wide spaces like an unbroken colt.
Shutting out all other thought, embalming the world

50 *1st Voice*: Sudden and sharp as an expletive

2nd Voice: As comforting as a carol of children

1st Voice: As stunning as a nuclear device.

2nd Voice: And when it passed, sulking away
Beyond the farther hill . . .

Narrator: It left a lightness
            In men's ears, a trembling lilt upon the lips,
            A glow on the heart's ebb, and men
            Smiled at the grateful blessing that is rain

Both Voices: The grateful blessing that is rain.

A. N. Forde
b. BARBADOS 1923

An Old Woman

            All other trees were clothed in leaves,
            But gaunt against the staring moon
            The cashaw thrust its ragged limbs,
            Each impotent,
       5   Since life had fled;
            And silent midst the laughing youth
            I saw her gnarled and ancient face,
            Expressionless and dead.

P. M. Sherlock
b. JAMAICA 1902

March Trades

            Earth leans the arctic
            Once more to the sun
            As the fond lover
            After anger's done
       5   Returns unto the loved one.
            In the north temperate zone
            Spring is being born;

And in our ever glittering
Torrid center
10 The trade winds wake
And shake their mane
On earth and ocean.
Fast flows the long green wave
Hurried by their urge
15 To crash their flowing strength
On furrowed rock and shoaling sand,
But strong is buttressed
Continent and island,
Sturdier than savagery of wind and sun.

20 Cumuli are shredded
Into flying fluffs
That scud like powder puffs
Tossed to the gale
Are driven from the boughs
25 Leaves ochreous
Of cedar, plum and shrub,
And fronded palms are fretted.
In village dooryards
And in close cool orchards
30 Perennial hardy mangoes
Bloom thick cream,
But the winds shear them
As they shear the fire from Immortelles
To startle the dark wood,
35 As they shear sheath from bud
And seed from shattered pod.
Close eastern windows
While the high wind blows
Too wildly in the eaves
40 And curtains fill like sails
And the rooms fret like cabins
Of gale gripped galleons.
Make all ship-shape

In stubborn Colon's simple way,
45   In the black slave-traders way,
In buccaneer and pirate way;
In the sturdy sea tramp's way;
Make all ship-shape,
For here on the rugged map
50   Of the Caribbean
Hurricane center shifts across meridians;
Jagged lightnings dart
Thunders roll and roar
Under close cloud ceilings
55   While barometers lower.
Let all be girt
In sinew, heart and spirit
To take the buffet
And to prosper in it.

Eric Roach
b. TOBAGO 1915 d. 1974

Growing Up

Children Coming from School

I can hear the gospel
Of little feet
Go choiring
Down the dusty asphalt street.

5 Beneath the vast
Cathedral of sky
With the sun for steeple
Evangeling with laughter
Go the shining ones
10 The little people.

Roger Mais
b. JAMAICA 1905 d. 1955

Still Life

A lizard sleeps upon the window-bar;
the window-curtains fold in sleep
their creeping jungles of convolvulus.
The noonday sun lies shadowless
5   with all its gold upon the trees –
their reds upon the sky like pain.
And sea and sky are one transparency –
a linen cloud, a sail
down-bellied in the calm.
0   Matisse might sketch his name upon the side
as though such patterns were the artist's theme.
But I shall call it still my own.
I saw it in the Indies
Not three days before I left.

Geoffrey Drayton
b. BARBADOS 1924

Adam and Batto

I
Adam now with his back to the land and the house where he lived
   saw the grin
flash bright from this rock that could fight this shark that could
   bite

5   his skin which on the beach was hard and rough and was spotted
   with salt
till it flaked like scales was smooth in the water and tight in the
   wind
and could carry a picture like a motorcar shine

10 and the sun was a medal on batto's chest
as he raised himself like water in wind
and his hands went high and quick quick quick as a hen does peck
they fell like a beak on adam's neck

it was bad bad bad as the sky went out and the water was flame
15 over adam's eyes glass winked like a fallen star on the sand
and a shadow of garfish passed like a cloud
as batto held him down with his knees and his glittering weight

II
with his back to the land and the house where he lived
adam wondered what
20 his mother would say if he didn't come back

and he thought of himself running up de black steps
the next day late for
school late for lunch late for

but if that was so he wouldn't be dead adam thought

III
25 and adam thought of x/mas day watching his father open the
wine, taking
the bottle between his knees his father had pulled till the cork
went pop
now he was the battle between batto's knees and this pushing for
30 breath was
the pull on the screw

but batto was shark in the bottle neck that kept bright hold on the
screw

IV
and adam can swim my sister will shout as i scatter the water
35 *about ... about ...*

V
as batto ducked him again

. VI

but this time adam touched adam caught adam held this boy who
was trying to beat him out of the water, looking back through the

blinding him bubbles he struck like a shark at the sea-egg shark's
belly pulled him down by the waist gripped his head and the grin

that was like a fire till they both dropped down together

beach boy and the boy who would be boy like the beach boys
were locked in the only way in the bay that could bring him his
spurs

and this was his wish as they hit the sand
and both were bottles at the floor of the bay

give in batto signalled
as the sky turned silver and the two lost time

give in batto signalled
as the ticking foam curled around them like vines

give in batto called
tugging at adam

lemme go lemme go lemme go

but adam held on and wouldnt let him go

Edward Brathwaite
b. BARBADOS 1930

St. Mary's Estate

They left remnants of the holocaust
in two long barracks guarding the mud road.
They left a tamarind tree,
branches bent like ears
5 · attuned, accustomed to sorrow.
They left cousin Johnny blind
sitting from morning till night,
wisdom too late, resignation
etched into his wooden visage.
10 Gangadia, gray hair, grandmother
genuflecting before Krishna,
towards the east,
contemplating nirvana,
imparting to young hooligans
15 the art of Hindi cuss.
They left a corbeau
in the middle of a dirt track
saying prayers
over the entrails of a dead ass.
20 They left and the sea
blew in
an inquisitive wind
who passed through the jalousies,
ruffled the now tender yellowing gazette,
25 modestly separating
neighbour from neighbour,
loitered on midday grimaces
that did not change
just because they left
30 Missy Moreau, aged,
chewing incantations
to the short memory
of ancestor and god, Shango.

Swifted away,
35   from St. Mary's Estate,
        on clandestine glances,
        They left sidestepping
        pebbles of goat shit
        and Papa, overseer, quiescent, tall.
40   On a spectral horse,
        who took respite
        in amber frothy urine,
        drowning the flowering bougainvillea.

Dionne Brand
b. TRINIDAD 1953

Encounters

Birthday Poem

for Clifford Sealy

To-day I would remember you whom birth brought no lucky dip
From which to pluck a permanent privilege,
And pain pushed prematurely into prose.
The photograph that recreates a child whose glance
5 Cast on the rescuing rock reads tyranny
His body bare to the bellowing wind
Has proved your former existence,
So when the season of awareness came
Passion made politics a serious game
10 And poverty your partner. How well I understood
The intolerant gesture, the juvenile lust to murder
An evil that had forged your life.

My birth records a similar story:
The freezing bastardy, the huddled tenantry,
15 Where children carry parents' pains like a uniform
Articulate only in their loyalty to life,
The individual desire or despair mocking most faithfully
Barometers that measure another's will,
And happiness as time indeed has shown
20 Absolved by the evil, intelligent question:
Was that piece of land a paying concern?

Those who start life without a beginning
Must always recall their crumbling foundations,
Rushing past affliction of the womb's unfortunate opening,

5 Reconsider now and again their earliest ambitions,
Or poised somewhere between loss and a possible arrival
Question their precarious present portion.
What new fevers arise to reverse the crawl
Our islands make towards their spiritual extinction?
10 Do you still patrol the city's unsavoury sites
Probing the prostitutes' hearts? Setting your intelligence
An exercise in pity as the warm nights
Drift their human flotsam before your questioning glance?

Nothing is changed in the news that reaches me here:
15 Papers continue to print the impossible, and rumours telegraph
Whatever falls within the senses' gauge.
Young poets are decorated with foreign approval
For precocious statements in a borrowed language,
Fashionable women whom comfort couldn't bless with sense
20 Still flock to applaud lectures by men
Who've a soft spot for the sound of their voices,
Corruption is keen; time throbs
With the ache of the proud and the sensitive like you
Who angrily wade through the vacuum
25 Forever afloat with oily seas,
While politicians posing incredible paunches
Parading their magical and primitive power
Fit the incompetent into jobs.

Life is similar in (what some call) the Mother Country
30 Where our people wear professions like a hat
That cannot prove what the head contains,
Success knows what grimace to assume,
Mediocrity is informed by a bright sense of bluff,
And Democracy a convenient attitude for many.
35 Students whom the huge city has shorn of glamour
Divorced from their status by a defect of colour
Find consolation in Saturday nights
With eloquent white whores that dance;
Or at nightfall over their new habit of tea
40 Argue with an elephant's lack of intelligence
Our culture must be spelt with a West Indian C.

We must suffer in patience whom life received
On islands cramped with disease no economy can cure,
Go with or without our lovers to the quiet shore
65 Where the reticent water weaves its pattern
And crabs crawl with a peculiar contemplation of the land,
Move through the multitude's monotonous cry
For freedom and politics at the price of blood,
Yet live every moment in the soul's devouring flame,
70 Until we fold with the folding earth,
Erect our final farewell in tree or cloud.
Hoping (if possible) for a people's new birth.

So you who care little for festival,
The seasonal sports, the carnival
75 Of barren souls in the February noon,
Preferring to inhabit your room, hoping to lean
On some durable solace in pages that justify
Your honest but innocent worship of the Russian regime
May not question why your exiled friend,
80 Seldom at ease in the habits of his time,
Never understanding why people pretend
To manufacture good wishes at certain times of the year,
Should yet try sincerely to offer you
A gift in words on your birthday.

George W. Lamming
b. BARBADOS 1927

Letter to Lamming in England

Older than you and cooler, more content,
I hold my narrow island in my hand
While you have thrown yours to the sea
And jumped for England, where, beyond my gaze,
5   I hear only your seasonal voice,
A lonely seagull's, crying on Atlantic.

My brother's is an echo's voice,
But love leans out to exile as to love
Lost or to the lately dead;
10   Forgive the thought divining you unhappy
In the vast alien city,
Aliened by our prohibited complexion,
Hungry in bone and spirit.

Forgive the dream that drags you back to islands
15   Desiring your genius home again
Among the immortelles and poincianas
Dropping red pathos on our naked graves;
Among our peasants barefoot as their cattle
In the intemperate weathers of our days.

20   Here in my dooryard's naked indigence
Hard labour bruises and lays bare the bone
Bent down for bare existence to the stone.
In shanty towns is hunger harsh, immoral,
The ladies of the dark parade their ware,
25   And ulcerous Lazarus groaning in the ghetto
Stodges a filthy offal not for dogs;
Oh for your oratory for the stricken dumb.

Our islands still are greener than we know them,
Our hopes are jungles of quick, turbulent growth;
30   In skulls as fossil as the wrath of slaves
Our ranting politicians pour foul potions
Poisoning the innocent good.

We are enslaved in the ancestral cane
We're trapped in our inheritance of lust,
35 The brown boot scorns the black,
And skins not white as white
Deny the black old matriarch in the cupboard.

Does winter prick the marrow as your dreams –
Classic images of hunger dancing
40 To reiterated rhythms drumming blood,
Hungry children skipping back to school,
Wrinkled and gnarled grandmothers crouched to chores
That children of the prodigals should eat,
Harsh laughter lapping up the streams of tears –
45 Do these stark patterns break the estranged heart,
Or does the banked Atlantic mar their passage?

Why were we born under the star of rhyme
Among a displaced people lost on islands
Where all time past is knotted in time present?
50 Here we are architects with no tradition,
Are hapless builders upon no foundation;
No skilled surveyors mark our forward road.
Can we speed through a score of centuries gone,
Leap from the sheer escarpment of our time
55 And mount like eagles proud-winged among eagles?

Here by the sea I sweat in prayer for you
Watching your kestrel way
Across that sky and climate, man of islands.
Remember cadences of island patois,
60 Old men's goatskin drumming,
Young men's tin percussion,
The sun's rose ruddy in our blood,
The wine excitement of our island women;
O man, your roots are tapped into this soil,
65 Your song is water wizard from these rocks.

Eric Roach
b. TOBAGO 1915 d. 1974

The Almond Trees

There's nothing here
this early;
cold sand
cold churning ocean, the Atlantic,
5   no visible history,

except this stand
of twisted, coppery, sea-almond trees
their shining postures surely
bent as metal, and one

10   foam-haired, salt-grizzled fisherman,
his mongrel growling, whirling on the stick
he pitches him; its spinning rays
'no visible history'
until their lengthened shapes amaze the sun.

15   By noon,
this further shore of Africa is strewn
with the forked limbs of girls toasting their flesh
in scarves, sunglasses, Pompeian bikinis,
brown daphnes, laurels, they'll all have
20   like their originals, their sacred grove:
this frieze
of twisted, coppery, sea-almond trees.

The fierce acetylene air
has singed

25   their writhing trunks with rust, the same
hues as a foundered, peeling barge.
It'll sear a pale skin copper with its flame.

The sand's white-hot ash underheel,
but their aged limbs have got their brazen sheen
30   from fire. Their bodies fiercely shine!
They're cured,
they endured their furnace.

Aged trees and oiled limbs share a common colour!

Welded in one flame,
35 huddling naked, stripped of their name,
for Greek or Roman tags, they were lashed
raw by wind, washed
out with salt and fire-dried,
bitterly nourished where their branches died,

40 their leaves' broad dialect a coarse,
enduring sound
they shared together.

Not as some running hamadryad's cries
rooted, broke slowly into leaf
45 her nipples peaking to smooth, wooden boles
their grief
howls seaward through charred, ravaged holes.

One sunburnt body now acknowledges
that past and its own metamorphosis
50 as, moving from the sun, she kneels to spread
her wrap within the bent arms of this grove
that grieves in silence, like parental love.

Derek Walcott
b. ST. LUCIA 1930

Colonisation in Reverse

Wat a joyful news, Miss Mattie,
I feel like me heart gwine burs'
Jamaica people colonizin
Englan in reverse.

5 By de hundred, by de t'ousan
From country and from town,
By de ship-load, by de plane-load
Jamaica is Englan boun.

Dem a-pour out o'Jamaica,
10 Everybody future plan
Is fe get a big-time job
An settle in de mother lan.

What a islan! What a people!
Man an woman, old and young
15 Jusa pack dem bag an baggage
An tun history upside dung!

Some people don't like travel,
But fe show dem loyalty
Dem all a-open up cheap-fare-
20 To-Englan agency.

An week by week dem shippin off
Dem countryman like fire,
Fe immigrate an populate
De seat o' de Empire.

25 Oonoo see how life is funny,
Oonoo see de tunabout,
Jamaica live fe box bread
Outa English people mout'.

For wen dem catch a Englan,
30 An start play dem different role,
Some will settle down to work
An some will settle fe de dole.

Jane say de dole is not too bad
Bacause dey payin she
35 Two pounds a week fe seek a job
Dat suit her dignity.

Me say Jane will never find work
At the rate how she dah look,
For all day she stay pon Aunt Fan couch
40 And read love-story book.

Wat a devilment a Englan!
Dem face war an brave de worse,
But I'm wonderin how dem gwine stan
Colonizin in reverse.

Louise Bennett
b. JAMAICA 1919

His Nerves Scraped White

And with his nerves scraped white
like Spanish Nettle
noise worries him

the growing islands he would work
5 for, worry him. Fishermen have loud rash voices;

on the sanded floor
feet scrape illiterate in the liquor
shop. Behind the door

10 he closed in vain – noise
worried him – the children scamper
round a happy ball: ex-

citements crawling over carpets,
armchairs and the other dozen vexed
15 and glued-together sticks

of hire-purchased furn-
iture that trip and trick
them, term-

inate their game. Noise
20 worried him. E-
rect, straight backed, their dun-

lopillow bottoms bound
in strict imported gir-
dles, the limbo loving girls

25 he loved, stepped
on the pavements in stil-
etto heels, tipp-

ing staccato over orange
peel. Sucked dry as that same orange
30 peel by his new dusty city,

his knuckles clutching tight
in padded purring cars,
he watches, glowing slow-
ly mad, the awe-
35 tomatic traffic lights: red
hot, the too slow

green gored
by electric horns.
This was the land-

40 scape where his fears
were born; here
the sick stalk, torn

of its tugging hope,
could not escape
45 the blazing season's fe-

ver; trees, covered walks,
dark mango alley-
ways, the love of jerk-

pork, snow-ball, souse,
50 small wooden houses
with their step-

up stones, were ruined in the glare.
Now slave no more
now harbour-

55 less no more, he forges
from his progress'
flames, new iron masters;

brilliant concrete crosses –
look – he bears – to crucify his freedom.
60 So he must cut the cane-

fields of Caymanas down,
of Chaguaramas down:
the soil too soiled

with whip, with toil,
65 with memory, with dust; replacing them with soil-

less, stain-
less, name-
less stalks

70 of steel like New
York, Paris,
London town.

Edward Brathwaite
b. BARBADOS1930

Men and Women

Since You

Since you,
I passed some nights in hell,
thought of destroying myself,
then thought of destroying you.
5   Panicked, took an iron bird
on some dragon cloud,
and flew from summer to summer,
till tiring we landed
where demon shadows eat away at my sleep.
10 Since you,
I walked miles and miles with a close friend,
listened for hours to street cars passing by,
talked rivers and rivers to find myself,
climbed twenty hills to take one breath.
15 Since you,
I bought a painting,
wrote a verse,
devoured many books,
hung out with friends,
20 lived a whole year,
never once discovering
that you weren't there.

Dionne Brand
b. TRINIDAD 1953

Villanelle of the Year's End

To an English lady; from a Jamaican. December 1983.

This is the year's end; cold winds blow.
Your fields burn frost-white; mine blaze red.
I have Poinsettia; you have snow.

The rich Poinsettia-colours flow
5   As if from heart's flood they had bled.
This is the year's end; cold winds blow.

From warm, sweet roots Poinsettias grow.
To clear bright Springs ice-frosts have led.
I have Poinsettia; you have snow.

10   What comes to bloom is what we sow:
is not love due to whom we wed?
This is the year's end; cold winds blow.

What use has storm when flame burns low?
What warmth the nightmare single bed?
15   I have Poinsettia; you have snow.

Four thousand miles of sea I know
Do not outdeep the tears we shed.
This is the year's end; cold winds blow.
I have Pointsettia; you have snow.

A. L. Hendriks
b. JAMAICA 1922

A Family Man

At night when the ordinary loves have settled
like dust drifting a little in my son's cough, my wife's
      breath, my daughter's sigh,
I call them in. From the dark side of leaves,
5 from the countries of desire, from the cracks in the road,
from the places I went to and never gave back
at the border, the faces I wanted and never forgave
for dying, from the dark side of leaves, they come
softer than smoke, shadows on paper,
10 like dust drifting a little in my wife's cough, my son's
      sigh, my daughter's breath.
They make hoarse journeys in my head. They cry
at the lamp's white pain. I silence them.
They orbit, tongueless. They die like stars; they cool
15 to ash. I trace their stain on paper, and sign it.
      Watch them
wind my life down like small, burnt moons. Watch them
      fall
like dust drifting a little in my daughter's cough, my wife's
20   sigh, my son's breath.

Dennis Scott
b. JAMAICA 1939

At two o'clock . . . .

At two o'clock in the morning
Darkness dissolves the room.

Your limbs lie still;
And, veiling your body in its mystery,
5 Darkness is a black shroud
Light and diffused as a wreath's perfume.

Till slowly, darkness enters your body,
And rocks in you
With the long, deep swell of ocean waves.
10 Outside
The wind whimpers in the trees.

The night is tortured;
Ruthlessly, it is chipped,
Chipped and splintered –
15 The silence split
Into a million pieces
By a pipe that drips.
Now in your loneness
The darkness begins
20 To pick at your mind
With bony fingers.

You are alone.
Between you
And that other body upon the bed
25 Distance is hard and tangible.
The soul cannot be reached;
It is a kernel, hidden far
Within its separate nut of sleep.

Outside
30 A jumbie bird mourns . . .

Loneliness,
Harsh as sandpaper,
Scrapes the heart.

Judy Miles
b. TRINIDAD 1944

The Sea and the Hills (1951)

For Jo:

Waves slithering over brown-skinned rock,
Hissing of waves as they mount the rocks–
By a pool appropriate with coral,
Caught in a column of sunlight I see you.
5 A girl, and yet more goddess than girl,
Brittle in beauty and bright as coral,
And words rage in my heart's darkness.
Midst the sibilant statements of the waves
A voice calling back from the future
10 Skewers the heart on a shaft of love
The perennial pain no prayer assuages–
The sunlight fades, the vision perishes,
All is darkness.

          But that was another day.
15 Hillside studded with rocks and bramble,
Brambles bristling with blackbirds–
And I have come into these high hills today
For I would carve you a song.
I am out of the sound of the sea,
20 I have come into these bird-infested hills
For today is a day of prayer and praise
And I would carve you a song
More lasting than marble, more beautiful
Than any goddess caught in alabaster.
25 But rock-coloured girl first tell me
Was it you that I saw? was it you?
Was yours the bird-shaped voice that called me?
Or was it some goddess trapped in the coral
Confined in rock for an ancient wrong
36 Turning in pain as the waves tormented her?
Goddess or girl, (to be sure, I know not
But) whichever you are, (wherever you are,) hear me:

From high on this heavenward hill
I gaze in the bay below me
35 Where waves, instinct with violence
Crawl towards the woman-bearing rocks,
And wishing to thank you (my girl, my goddess,
Who brings me back my singing voice
Though afraid of the smart of the aching blood)
40 From the crest of my love I shape you this prayer:
Though a poet approach her rayed in love,
His fond, fond words, through her foliage of flesh,
Through her branching veins, swiftly winging,
May her arms never know the torment
45 Of encircling this obdurate lover
For his heart is ringed round with raging words
And his grief is as old as Adam and Eve.
If she, embayed in his arms,
Turn in pain and cry for the moon,
50 Though her crime be as ancient as woman,
O let her not know confinement in rock
For the sea is within us, is intractable,
Rages in a twitch of the heart and traps us
With promises of a more auspicious season;
55 And all men know that the too hot heart
Shall ache into stone ere this ancient rock
Chafes into blood once more.

The prayer ends,
Vision and sunlight (are shattered
60 by the raging dark).

Cecil Herbert
b. TRINIDAD 1926

I Have Survived So Long

Love, love, I have survived so long
upon the naked bed of your unconcern.
But I am learning your roster:
the bugle call at dawn,
5 your gate-shutting rites,
the changing of the guard.
Circumspect inside, you inspect
your pleated ranks, the chessmen
from your peopled platoon stuck
10 upon the iron squares of your strategy.
You sit, your chin
upon your hand, like history,
contemplating boundaries.
But only new time
15 can be your adequate mistress.
The days are miserly, the hours
thin and vaporless, the new season a dream.

I am the insurrection
your strong hand put down; the cry
20 and the blade in the sunlight,
the nascent moon-threads
of the garment of dreams,
the unpaged history of you and I,
the beautiful moon-child
25 whose cry I always hear.
They have not dealt with me yet: your squad.
Their bullets get wet, they
change their guards. Had I stood
against the wall of my courage,
30 or had they fired at the dutiful
hour, it would have been
final.

I would have won
the case of my belief.
35 Instead, this
wretched sentence exiling me
to memory.

Mahadai Das
b. GUYANA

Horses

*(Young men once described their women as
'Tanks' and 'Horses')*

Sitting near the harbour
looking out to sea
at ships & nights that brought you friends
from lands
5 you've never even seen

Just looking at your untamed ways
made a rage then grow within
your velvet moonlit body swayed
as the bow came closer in

10 My hurt would ride on waves
if my days could find your thirst
O, to be the well
from which you drank
though I'd never be there first

15 Like a dying tree
I stood there saddened
parched with shedding bark
your graceful hips moved hearing
grinning voices in the dark

20   Making hooves of twelve wild stallions
thunder across my chest
I watched them reach into your bosom
& take a scarlet scarf from out your breast.

Your bangles jingled loudly
25   waving at the crew
& they in turn blew vile kisses
making funny signs at you

They swept you up alaughing
in smelly tattooed arms
30   waves grew high & stormy
as they rubbed against your charms

One sailor
was from Middlesex
he waved his back at me
35   I told myself just then & there
This ain't the place to be.

You though,
found what you were after
you drank a passion wine
40   they kissed your neck against the mast
as groans rocked this heart of mine

You cried in pain
wept aloud
smashed against the rock
45   I cursed to think I'm not the well
where, in thirst,
you'd dip your cup

It took wines of kinds
& crescent nuts to save me
50   from that mire
& red horses with golden manes
to save me from the fire

Took the eyes of lakes & sleep & sea
to cease the sounds I'd heard
55 & woke with woe next morning
from dogs & drunks I'd turned.

O Goddess of this island
giving sunshine pearls to guests

O velvet queen of sequin worlds
60 in your skin-black satin dress

Come
let me be your waters
these nights they make you blind
walk with me to this dreamer's house
65 to see the life you'd find

With toil I'd bring silk curtains
through which palm winds blow
& for you a gown of lace
where only joys could flow

70 O, never mind the harbour
today's tomorrow's past
let me be your laughter
let me be the last.

Now
75 you evil fog horn,
sail on from my bay
& let me take this moonlight
to walk my love away.

Dawad Philip
b. TRINIDAD & TOBAGO

The Catherine Letter

Strange   my writing to you

Can I say a cliché

Never thought I would see the day when you would cut me   glimpsed
you in   should have said at   should have said near   a bank one day; smiled
5   waved; and you cut me

Catherine   name from the north

Well   there's a mystery to women of frost   the young men stride to the
woods and snip them dark lilacs   a wren wheels in the distance   the sun
shells east of the lake

10   Couples kiss in the field across the wild cherries

In the dream the woman is sitting under a cotton   a man kneels on the
slope   the pair meet in the mist, stuttering prayers

Have you seen lilies tilt in the wind

Do banks stretch shadows on people so that when they see the familiar
15   they turn away

Sometimes roses mistake violets for other flowers   Do you think there
will ever be concert between men and women   Catherine   sad   in
September

Some names sing in the air like lit swans

20   Catherine   name like a fir

The leaves turn with a fine cadence   The dancers touch hands under the
elms

Critic one   is this a letter or a poem

Critic two   surrealist nonsense

25   Critic three   language in dream sequence

I cry to the stones because I am lonely, the girl said to the dark

Perhaps if I look through this file I will find her charred letter

Catherine and Natalie, moving

The most beauteous virgin weeps in the rain

30   Catherine   if I talked to a fern do you think it would
answer   if I stopped at your window what

Hyacinths   I dial a number   soft click

A thrush glides in slow circles over the brook

Catherine stands by the fence, watching a leopard

35   I call you from fire   in the white wheel

I give you the valley

Tony McNeill

Anthony McNeill
b. JAMAICA 1941

Quadrille for Tigers

In all your straight lines
I curve trying to find
a little hollow
a gap under the window
5 through which to climb
into your friendship.

On the cool slope
of white hibiscus
a humming bird
10 shakes his emerald glow
and sits, small head tilted.
How easy his poise
how sweet their stillness.

In the streets and broken houses
15 we put our thorns first.
Harsh words roll along the cracks,
harsher thoughts drip from reddened eyes
as every day we turn a knife
between our apathy and anger.

20 Between the noise and silence
we move in careful steps
each with too much past unsorted
for brisker measure. But I am weary
of this slow quadrille, for tigers
25 leap behind my clouded brain
spiders stretch their furry joints
ready to trip me out of step.

Christine Craig
b. JAMAICA

Elemental

I would have words as tenacious as mules
to bear us, sure-footed
up the mountain of night

to where, at daybreak,
5 we would shake hands with the sun
and breathe the breezes of the farthest ocean

and, as we descended,
in sunlight,
We would be amazed
10 to see what hazards we had passed.

Edward Baugh
b. JAMAICA 1936

The Black Tree

He stood with the woman in his arms
where the lane, veering, plunged its black
snakeskin gleam smoothly between sentries of amber
till it lost volition to an amber haze
5 and felt his blood thicken.
                    He listened,
as a tree listens
for the lightest stirrings of its nerves
at the midges' news, through the cavernous roar
10 of sap in its slow veins,

and as the woman in his arms
buried her face against the glare
of headlamps lunging sideways from their high cave,
he heard, distinctly as a tree hears
15 rain in the black hills feelering near,
the tumult of approaching war,

and he saw Earth as she would be
when it was done: weak, grinning and
dazedly rising, but still one
20   with the ponderous, serene and stoneblind spheres.

These things he felt, heard and saw
in his thirty-sixth year,
standing, without fear or hope,
with a girl from his island quiet in his arms,

25   beneath pale cloud, in Europe.

Wayne Brown
b. TRINIDAD 1944

Politics and Society

I Write About

You ask: Why do you write
so much about blood, sweat & tears?
Don't you write about trees, flowers,
birds, love?

5   Yes

I write about trees –
trees with withered branches
& severed roots

I write about flowers –
10 flowers on graves

I write about birds –
caged birds struggling

I write about love –
love for destruction
15 of oppression

Orlando Wong
b. JAMAICA 1952

The Slums

In the slums
Jewel staring eyes
Of human flies
Crowd the rims
5 Of our social order.
We avoid
The stench of slums
Everything uncomfortable
Insistence
10 Of staring eyes
Evidence
Of substanceless limbs.

Here are –
Bilious houses
15 At the womb-head
Of comfort
Riches
Pleasure.

Here are –
20 Magnificent skeletons
With shrinking skins
Shrinking
With our approval.
Here
25 Here is
The world we accept
From our glass houses.

George Campbell
b. JAMAICA 1916

from Sappho Sakyi's Meditations

I
Like sun-
Rise
The Wise
Old spider
5   Comes
Into view.

Bone-
Less
His
10   Brain in
His belly
He is

The perfect
Philosopher.
15   Thread-
Spinning Socrates
And that other
Fellow

Who
20   Lived in his
Tub
Might
Easily have become
Spiders.

III
25   Shamba Bolongongo, the Bushongo King of the Congo
Patron of arts and a preacher of peace
Abolished in war the use of dangerous
Weapons and drugs, instructing his soldiers carefully only to wound.

30   Even this king, it appears, would have come
To agree to the limited use of the hydrogen bomb.

IV
While we move forward into space
The deep-sea Angler-Fish, as weird
As any robot-ship the planeteers have
Planned, squats patiently among the nether
35   Bracken of the tide. Pouched frog-
Headed, Humpty-Dumpty-round around
The mouth, horned like a basilisk,
Determined as an owl, this ghoul-eyed
Monster lights a lovely lantern to attract
40   Those unsuspecting, unsophisticated fish
That wish that such extravagance were theirs;
And like the victims of the legendary Siren's song
They find too late that lovely sights and curious
Sounds lie washed around and governed by
45   Insatiable shipwreck rocks. Our
Inter-planetary suitors, then, might well
Consider, in their snout-nosed ships,
The deep-sea Angler-Fish
Who moves through darkest subdiluvial space
50   With crew of permanently fixed and shrunken
Parasitic husbands for her mates.

VIII
Puffins and penguins
In their flocks resemble
Certain loquacious market women,

55   After the business of the mating season
These matrons gravely re-assemble
With murderous mumble

To discuss their men.
A single syllable will unsettle ten
60   Smug husbands who thought themselves secure

And with a shrug or grumble
They can strip a humble lover
To the bone.

No wonder
65 That the little spider
Lives alone.

EPILOGUE
Sappho Sakyi
Had a weary
Way of saying
70 What was true

Sappho Sakyi
Had a weary
Way of saying
What was true

75 Because he knew
A multitude
Of raven's feathers
Could not restrain the sky from being blue.

He'd examined every raven's feather
80 So he knew.

Edward Brathwaite
b. BARBADOS 1930

Dutty Tough

Sun a shine but tings no bright;
Doah pot a bwile, bickle no nuff;
River flood but water scarce, yaw;
Rain a fall but dutty tough.

5 Tings so bad dat nowadays when
Yuh ask smaddy how dem do
Dem fraid yuh teck it tell dem back,
So dem no answer yuh.

No care omuch we dah work fa
10 Hard-time still eena we shut;
We dah fight, Hard-time a beat we,
Dem might raise we wages, but

One poun gawn awn pon we pay, an
We no feel no merriment
15 For ten poun gawn awn pon we food
An ten poun pon we rent!

Salfish gawn up, mackerel gawn up,
Pork an beef gawn up same way,
An when rice an butter ready
20 Dem just go pon holiday!

Claht, boot, pin an needle gawn up;
Ice, bread, taxes, water-rate;
Kersene ile, gasolene, gawn up;
An de pound devaluate.

Louise Bennett
b. JAMAICA 1919

Afternoon Elegy

The land is full of echoes; all the bright
company of men the dumb
land uttered in prophesying tongues are gathered
in the constant afternoon. Flame licks the hills. It
5   is enough that I am here, one
with the maimed and dead and utterly victorious
citizens of the moment. Here is perfection in a
calm miniature of hills, the leaden
sea, the desolate street, the tidy
10   burgher addressing himself to evening
and the suburbs. Day is shuttered
and done. Who is lonely
as the Wind? None sees his shadow.

Basil McFarlane
b. JAMAICA 1922

Caribbean Basin

Islands described as emerald border
this sea where once before piracy was law.
This basin that the present predators
slit with their fins like periscopes once saw
5   swift rape of gaping children just as green
with innocence. Their awe they gave as welcome,
but when the reek of blood brought cognisance
of guns to make them glutton's prey their staves
and darts in answer fought the wind like straw.

10   Yet innocence persists like upturned keels
of boats that will not sink: hearts no less ripe
for pickings and invasions open up
to messages of iron on the waves;

tides bear the doctrine of the sharpened claw
15 in fresh assaults upon benevolence
and television's magic dupes them with its reels
of El Dorado bright with stars and stripes.

It is the age-old decoy for the poor:
the ship of bounty sailing in to shore
20 before the after-life which comes to strike
uneven distributions from the score.
Meanwhile they learn to emulate the shark
cruising with avarice at their open door
and turn away from socialistic crap.
25 You can't eat ideology, he said,
and with one swipe wiped Christ off the map.

Cecil Gray
b. TRINIDAD 1923

from Tales of the Islands

Chapter X

'adieu foulard . . .'
I watched the island narrowing the fine
Writing of foam around the precipices then
The roads as small and casual as twine
Thrown on its mountains; I watched till the plane
5 Turned to the final north and turned above
The open channel with the grey sea between
The fishermen's islets until all that I love
Folded in cloud; I watched the shallow green
That broke in places where there would be reef,
10 The silver glinting on the fuselage, each mile
Dividing us and all fidelity strained
Till space would snap it. Then, after a while
I thought of nothing, nothing, I prayed, would change;
When we set down at Seawell it had rained.

Derek Walcott
b. ST. LUCIA 1930

Homecoming: Anse La Raye

(for Garth St Omer)

Whatever else we learned
at school, like solemn Afro-Greeks eager for grades,
of Helen and the shades
of borrowed ancestors,
5   there are no rites
for those who have returned,
only, when her looms fade,
drilled in our skulls, the doom-
surge-haunted nights,
10   only this well-known passage
under the coconuts' salt-rusted
swords, these rotted
leathery sea-grapes leaves,
the seacrabs' brittle helmets, and
15   this barbecue of branches, like the ribs
of sacrificial oxen on scorched sand;
only this fish-gut reeking beach
whose spindly, sugar-headed children race
whose starved, pot-bellied children race
20   pelting up from the shallows
because your clothes,
your posture
seem a tourist's.
They swarm like flies
25   round your heart's sore.

Suffer them to come,
entering your needle's eye,
knowing whether they live or die,
what others make of life will pass them by
30   like that far silvery freighter
threading the horizon like a toy;

for once, like them,
you wanted no career
but this sheer light, this clear,
35 infinite, boring, paradisal sea,
but hoped it would mean something to declare
today, I am your poet, yours,
all this you knew,
but never guessed you'd come
40 to know there are homecomings without home.

You give them nothing.
Their curses melt in air.
The black cliffs scowl,
the ocean sucks its teeth,
45 like that dugout canoe
a drifting petal fallen in a cup,
with nothing but its image,
you sway, reflecting nothing.
The freighter's silvery ghost
50 is gone, the children gone.
Dazed by the sun
you trudge back to the village
past the white, salty esplanade
under whose palms, dead
55 fishermen move their draughts in shade,
crossing, eating their islands,
and one, with a politician's
ignorant, sweet smile, nods,
as if all fate
60 swayed in his lifted hand.

Derek Walcott
b. ST. LUCIA 1930

Black Friday 1962

were some who ran one way.
were some who ran another way.
were some who did not run at all.
were some who will not run again.
5 And I was with them all,
when the sun and streets exploded,
and a city of clerks
turned a city of men!
Was a day that had to come,
10 ever since the whole of a morning sky,
glowed red like glory,
over the tops of houses.

I would never have believed it,
I would have made a telling repudiation.
15 But I saw it myself
and hair was a mass of fire!
So now obsessed I celebrate in words
all origins of creation, whores and virgins:
I do it with a hand upon a groin,
20 swearing this way, since other ways are false!

For is only one way, one path, one road.
And nothing downward bends, but upward goes,
like leaves to sunlight, trees to the sun itself.
All, all who are human fail,
25 like bullets aimed at life,
or the dead who shoot and think themselves alive!

Behind a wall of stone beside this city,
mud is blue-grey when ocean waves are gone,
in the midday sun!
30 And I have seen some creatures rise from holes
and claw a triumph like a citizen,
and reign until the tide!

atop the iron tops of this city
I see the vultures practising to wait.
35   And everytime, and anytime,
in sleep or sudden wake, nightmare, dream,
always for me the same vision of cemeteries, slow funerals,
broken tombs, and death designing all

True, was with them all,
40   and told them more than once:
in despair there is hope, but there is none in death.
Now I repeat it here, feeling a waste of life,
in a market-place of doom, watching the human face!

Martin Carter
b. GUYANA 1927

Sacred Flame

Our women
the ones I left behind
always know the taste
of their own strength –
5   bitter at times it might
be

But I
armed only with
my mother's smile
10   must be forever gathering
my life together like scattered beads

What was your secret mother –
the one that made you a woman
and not just Akosua's wife

15   With your thighs you gave
a generation of beautiful children

With your mind you willed the crops
commanding a good harvest

With your hands and heart
20 plantain soup and love

But the sacred flame of your woman's
kra you gave to no man, mother

Perhaps that was the secret then–
the one that made you a woman
25 and not just Akosua's wife

Grace Nichols
b. GUYANA 1950

Creators

Trane

Propped against the crowded bar
he pours into the curved and silver horn
his old unhappy longing for a home

the dancers twist and turn
5   he leans and wishes he could burn
his memories to ashes like some old notorious emperor

of rome. but no stars blazed across the sky when he was born
no wise men found his hovel; this crowded bar
where dancers twist and turn,

10 holds all the fame and recognition he will ever earn
on earth or heaven. he leans against the bar
and pours his old unhappy longing in the saxophone

Edward Brathwaite
b. BARBADOS 1930

Birthday Poem

The summer that brings me
My fiftieth year
Brings me also
Yet another unfinished poem
5 A certificate of merit
Or two
No silver gold nor bronze

Fifty years of not quite
Gaining any thing
10 (But weight
And a chance of understanding
What it means to
Be nearly third
Best, regularly)

John Figueroa
b. JAMAICA 1920

This Poem

This poem contemplates a time
beyond the consoling agony of words.

I watched my father dying in bitterness,
I held his ankles as the cold crept close.

5 This poem turns frail eyes on emptiness
and keeps its peace.

I have seen the eyes of girls grow wide and world-illuminant
at smallest gestures of considerate love.

Hearing disorder gather to its thunderous head,
10 this poem tests its wings
and tunes its throat.

Edward Baugh
b. JAMAICA 1936

Portrayal

He sketched, then painted me –
Me poring on the keyboard of my pan,
My drumsticks poised to loosen melodies,
My arched wrists near the circle of the steel.
5 He must have felt the thrust of two-pronged chords
Piercing his soul. He must have held his breath
With mine at the keen edged flight of the notes
Flung from the quiver of my instrument.
The soft touch might have quelled him, and the lulls,
10 The many silences cause him to pause,
Dangling his brush, his art and mine together strung;
He one with me the whilst; his heart with mine now slung

How he mirrored me, knew my inmost self
And stamped it there! my brows frowned in the zeal,
15 Frowned in the pain of giving birth to song,
My down bent eyes that spoke a hundred things,
Dark histories of stirring fact and strength,
From lips that knew the sweet vernacular,
And felt the bruise oft-times of angry tones.
20 He read indeed that murder in my look
And told it with his brush, for I would slay
His soul with music, leave him spiritless and done,
But we were knit in being here: we two were one.

So I thrilled him to the core with music
25 Pulsing and sweet, wakening harmonies.
Dreams long forgotten, new hope bright as noon,
Soft sad threnodies, then gay themes that roused
Reminding him of clever dancing girls.
I shook him with a fury wild of airs,
30 The rhythms of my land, (I play all tunes).
He stopped and could not paint: He seemed bewitched.
Locked to this mood a while, he stayed, rocked with the sound
And beat a tango with a foot upon the ground.

My music was the sun, terrific, warm,
35 My music was the mild and mellow moon
My music was the twinkling April rain,
The sublety of night and spying stars,
The bleak sad face of dawns that change to light,
Hills green in ever level sea of peace,
40 Gay heart of city, sparkling lights and noise of steel,
The breathless agony of joy like that I feel.

His features moved with mine swayed by the spell
I wove with flailing sticks, hands and a heart;
Forehead to furrows creased and salt sweat oozed.
45 That power which was mine and surged in me
Stirred him where he stood like marionette,
Sensing the verve that worked me playing to a fill,
For magic had caught me, music had claimed my will.

I might have held him there, but in a hush,
50 He mastering began to paint again.
On canvas, all the grace in me he caught
The triumph hidden subtly in my mien.
Perhaps, he heard on Carnival above the row
My shout: 'Play music men, le's roll dem over now!'

55 He painted to an end, and there it was,
Immortal replica of me done while
I burnt with rapture from the sense of being great
Lightsome and blithe as spirit, buoyed in boundless state

Spirit I was, comrade of deathless might,
60 A daring flight of joy in moments freed from bond,
Far from the self I knew, removed, and quiet beyond.

Here was true image toned in colour warm and strong,
With written script beneath it: 'Soloist, Ping Pong'.

Owen Campbell
b. ST. VINCENT

The Hammer – *a calypso in four acts – sung by David Rudder*

Act 1: Scene 1: "The Wake".

Laventille here we come,
We're singing praises to your son,
Oh Laventille here we come.

5   Act 1: Scene 2: "The Happening".
Somewhere up in Laventille,
Many years ago,
A man had a hammer,
Used to follow him to and fro,
10 He used to use it to. . .
Pound a pan,
Or sometimes Rinda,
A stupid man,
All in the savannah,
15 Never miss Panorama,
One day the ole hammer just disappear, (oh)
Some say it vanish into thin air.

CHORUS:
Wey de man wid de hammer gone – Tell
20 me, tell me,
Wey he gone,

Anybody know wey de hammer gone –
Tell me, tell me,
Wey he gone,
25 Can you tell me what going on – Tell me,
tell me.
Wey he gone,
Ah want to know where de hammer gone
– Tell me, tell me,
30 Wey he gone.

Why you up and leave – Trail.
Why you make me grieve – Trail,
Hammer tell me flat – Trail,
Why yuh do we dat – Trail,
35 Well the dragon doh walk de trail no
more,
Well the dragon doh walk de trail no
more.

Act II: "The Passing".
40 From April of '85...,
Hammer went to sleep,
After years of making noise... (now)
Not even ah peep,
He used to move wid de dragon band
45 All thro' dis soca land,
Always on the scene,
They used to control the barber-greene,
Well de dragon doh walk de trail no more,
Who holding de hammer I want to know.

50 Act III: "The Funeral Scene"
On a silver chariot... riding,
To the sun,
Leaving fire in it's wake,
Spirits on the run,
55 And as we gather round that day,
Ah hear sister Sheila say,
How last night she "See ah sign",
She see the hammer and it,
"Doing fine." Same time thunder roll,
60 She bawl out, "yuh see,"
"He done start to tune the pan already".

CHORUS

Act IV: "Rudolph's Dream".
I want to hear the hammer ring out,
65 From every panyard and
From Europe to Africa,
Just like here in Trinidad,

This hammer must never die,
Let me tell yuh why,
70 Anytime de music dead,
Is then life go buss we head,
So the children start singing the refrain
desperately,
Begging me to ask the question again.

75 CHORUS

David Rudder
b. TRINIDAD

Road-Mending

Patches of black
In the pitch
Make the most
Unusual patterns:
5 Irregular blocks,
Birds' wings,
Shapes of ships,
Animals' heads,
Curiously
10 Interfigured.

This is the
Road-mender's art:
With tar and gravel
To design
15 A dozen or more
Shapes and figures:
To figure out
From fancy only
How to inlay
20 Gravel and tar . . . . .

Barnabas J. Ramon-Fortuné
b. TRINIDAD 1905

Le Petit Paysan

(Modigliani)

His shoes, which you can't see, the little peasant's,
Are huge with earth, and damp with season's rain.
He does not know of any world beyond his:
Soil, seeding, fruiting, and the soil again.

5   But in his eyes a certain shrewd assessment
Of weathers' change, and freckled starlight, glows.
His hands, at rest, have given massive blessing
To root and wildflower, cabbage leaf and rose.

It is quite strange to him to have to sit so;
10   Nor turn his head to watch a cart go by.
But he accepts the moment as it passes –
And does not dream that it will never die.

Barbara Ferland
b. JAMAICA 1919

Dilemmas

I Now Have Some Twenty Years

i now have some twenty years
in measured time strung out
and down the high tensioned road
there are some who lie sprawled and bleeding
5   in my ragged wake of passing
and some who sit softly weeping
for the speed of my passing
and yet many others who still stand
in silent grey positions
10   and lie waiting
for others to come stumbling
to slash and crush their bones
as they go running
as they struck and battered mine
15   with their heavy hidden weapons
of thoughts and words and ugly deeds
they stand and lie waiting
for others are sure to come
as we are an ageless line
20   who have no place to stand in time
measured long strung out
we are an endless line

and through it all
though the scars hang deep and long
25　my tongue has been untouched
and must silently sing out
when it will
of the quiet sounds within my mind
where no heavy club or sword
30　clutched in no grey hand
ever
can come near
and though it was not easy
and though the scars hang long and deep
35　my tongue has been unspoiled
and must silently sing out
when its hungry seeking eyes
draw out and softly touch
yet another silent ear

40 .　for we are an ageless line
we who have no room to stand
who need no room
who want no room to stand
or lie or sit or crawl around
45　in a heavy time measured grey and hung out
we are a long
and endless
moving
line

Michael Foster
b. BARBADOS 1945 d. 1965

The Castle

His mother told him of the king's
enormous thick-walled castle where
with lots of yellow courtiers
he kept his yellow court of fear.

5 The bold knight hopped a milk-white horse,
  spurred fiercely, keen as anything;
  resolved, this honourable knight,
  to slay that fearful king.

  The giddy knight rode hard and fast.
10 At dusk he heaved a dreadful sigh:
  at last, that frightful yellow flag
  against the darkening sky!

  LIVING IS FEARING. Tired, he read
  the writing on the castle wall,
15 and braced himself to slay that king
  who terrifies us all.

  The drawbridge down, the knight spurred hard,
  galloping into battle;
  but as he neared, the bridge pulled up
20 with a disdainful rattle.

  Too late to stop, he took the plunge;
  accoutred well, he couldn't float;
  and, loud exclaiming 'Death to Fear!',
  he drowned himself in the moat.

Mervyn Morris
b. JAMAICA 1937

The Stenographer

The simplicity of a rounded, pendant sorrow
Enhances the view from her window of the hills,
She sits on narrow, upright thighs, declaiming
Her high-church assignation, though perhaps it kills
5   The unstained green glass of the hills.

Her fingertips caress the black face of her master
Automatically. The hedge of margin bars
Her undictated thoughts, should they go straying
Unpunctuated. No error mars the white page
10   Of her mind. No asterisks. No stars.

Barbara Ferland
b. JAMAICA 1919

Because I have turned my back

Because I have turned my back
Upon those things,
Those hours,
The frail immemorial flowers
5   Sprung from the stillness
Where the will is of no avail,
No bird now sings.

Because I have set my face
Towards the endeavour,
10   Time's racing river,
And greet upon the street
The acquaintance, chance companion
And the city's minion,
The wires trill other messages;
15   And the still recollection
No more assuages.

Because I face a task
And wear a mask that takes
Root, and set my foot
20 Upon a pavement made with human hands,
And go where now
My need demands;

Because I have turned
From that unheeded shore,
25 I know no more
The wind that strikes along the wave
And the silent grove
Where peace burned
All day long.

30 But because I have known
Those things,
And felt their fingers wind
Their traceries within my mind,
My heart turns traitor, spurns
35 These hands, these eyes; yearns
To go back
Drift with the long
Slow sweep of the wave
Into the deep: leave
40 Me here
Without a heart
To grieve.

Frank Collymore
b. BARBADOS 1893 d. 1980

Compassionate Spider

There is a face in a coffin
three years
in my mind.

I have a tough projector
5   inside
with a life-guarantee on its label.

When the radio blasts
some tune from the dead,
my mind's taperecorder

10   finds the right spot
at 3¾ speed.
The guns shut down for the day, Miller and Shore on-

stage, adjust their mikes and prepare to
begin.
15   My comrades wait, who have shaved

for the occasion;
they stipple the mind like birds.
But look! something is lurking outside the pleasant

arena, *inches* away on tape.
20   At any minute, the film will shift
into black and white.

And listen!
a chorus of dogs brings back the guns
and the war's relived for the fiftieth time. Then,

25   with no button pressed, on to the latest victim
fastforward,
who lies my God! *just as he was* under the breath-stained glass

in St. Andrew Parish –
Held for ten seconds, then cut! and you're off on a new track.
30   The compassionate spider hurries the cobwebs back.

But someone has blown out his brains by then,
½-believing the thing was real.
Dead actors, also, may perform well.

Anthony McNeill
b. JAMAICA 1941

Suicide?

Seaweeds
sulk upon the rock;
black sand teems with stones.

Here
5 in this green and black holiday place
death is a white fowl, strangled,
slapping the eye.

Memory searches
the sea of the mind . . .
10 Until at last a barb of guilt
harpoons these hours to his face.

For when his heart, driven before a gale
of loneliness, sought in our hearts
a harbour and a home
15 no sign we gave
to anchor our compassion in his soul.

Not silence itself was our sin;
for touching hands
turn silence to a delicate
20 exquisite thing, slender
breath of a dawn campfire
on this beach; and eloquent
as a lone seagull's flight.

Why
25 is tenderness usually late
or, if it does come,
frail as foam?

Judy Miles
b. TRINIDAD 1944

Time, Folkways, Religion

I Cannot Bear . . .

I cannot bear that this girl's young sweet line
Must swell, be sucked and sag and that her hips
Must wrap their shapely arcs around with fat.

Why always must life thicken from her spring,
5   Her youth of slim and lovely April buds –
With wind for hair, and fragrance in her touch, –
So she must wedge her slack and bellying form
Within a corset?

        One would never dream
10 Seeing the laughing girls trip gaily by
That Time will throw its overcoat of age
And so obscure the youthful mould of beauty.

A. J. Seymour
b. GUYANA 1914

The Word Once Spoken

the word once spoken falls upon
the ground and instantly is gone

and like a star that burns, man comes,
clean as a word, or like a flame,

5   blazing, then instantly is gone
back into silence as he came –

only the breadth of a breath divides
the calm of the sea from the raging tides.

bloom, rose, within your blazing hour!
10   with darts of fragrance wound the spellbound air!

sing, furious bird, your furious song!
assault the ear of life with your sweet power!

sing now; bloom now: another sun will bring
another rose, another bird to sing. . . .

Barnabas J. Ramon-Fortuné
b. TRINIDAD 1917

Judas

That evening, not so long ago,
the Master, fingers in the dish,
said gently: 'Did I not choose
you twelve, yet one of you's
5   a devil?' Mocking, he glanced
at me; and others, quick
on cue, looked my way too.

The odd man out is always
Judas. 'We're from Galilee.'
10 (Nasty little province,
smells of fish!)

The point is,
Jesus never trusted me.
John, who's favourite, he's
15 from Galilee. Like Peter,
Andrew, all the cosy band.
Which Galilean, Lord,
will sit at your right hand?

Tonight I kissed him
20 and I saw
that mocking glance again.
'Betrayest thou the Master
with a kiss?' he said, ironic; then
seemed pleased or something
25 like relieved he'd got me
right. That knowing judge of men,
he surely ought to realize
that truths are often complicated:
what he spotted he created,
30 distrusting with those distant
foreign eyes.

The point is not the money. I'll
go give it back. For, hell,
what's thirty bits of silver?
35 I would not sell
the Master, he's for free. Just
preserve my purity of hate
for him I served and loved so well.
My Lord, the Master of my fate,
40 always withheld his trust.

Mervyn Morris
b. JAMAICA 1937

from Testament

A day ends and a way ends and a world ends here
A day ends and a way ends and a world ends here
And yet so sure the peace
So sure the peace
5 A day ends and a way ends and a world ends here.

in self-created blindness waits this earth
And all the peoples lost and shelterless
Stumbling amongst the ruins to the brink
Of utmost ruin. And the world ends here.
10 And yet so great the peace, this wind so sure
So strong so full of vision that the faith
Loses in last awareness of the source
The great pervading stillness of the root.
O be this pure, O be this free from fault
15 Of affectation or distrust or fraud
O be this like a flute upon thy lips
Prophetic Night to pour thy mighty hymn.

Old women in the gardens weeding grass
Old men along the quayside fly their rods
20 The cinemas, the slums and palaces
Declare and spawn the dozen deformed gods.
The builder plies his trowel. Ages pass.
The search receives the seeker. Time still nods.
O be for all this night the birth of faith
25 And light the road, and long the travelling.

There is a limit to all human ways
There is a limit to all human love
And a great darkness in all human light
Yet faith flows down the river, peace fills trees,
30 And glory lights the morning when she comes
All wet and radiant from the golden clouds
And walks upon the mountains like a bride.
For there is promise in all human pain

There is a morning in all human night
35   And life and birth and beauty beyond death.

We have constructed Time with fear and greed
We have imprisoned Space with avarice
And murdered Life, the Vision, with our Sloth
We have constructed Time
40   Constructed Time
We have created Death in all our walks.

M. G. Smith
b. JAMAICA 1921

The Visit

The keskidee calls stubbornly
from the lianas.
A scramble of brambles

tries the shut door.
5   Nobody in.
Perhaps there's been a gold rush

or something.
This is a dead town.
But there's this clock

10   still ticking.
And there's this stable
with the fresh smell of dung.

Perhaps they'll be back
soon.
15   So the stranger on horseback, in formal black,

waited, with an emissary's
patience, while
the clock tocked and the stable dried,

the worms gained and even the door
20 fell in suddenly, on a clean, well-lighted
place –

then, as great birds came gliding in
through the stretched jaws
of the valley,

25 he was sure, and he turned,
slapped leather twice
and rode off, his slowly-cantering horse

raising no echoes nor planting the least
hoofprints in the indifferent clay.

Wayne Brown
b. TRINIDAD 1944

Letter for a Friend

I
It is not always dark
Often I have seen day with dawn
Like a rag dusting out the night
And the stars retreat into the deep sky;
5 Seen the houses come out of hiding
And the day awake, shake itself,
Resume its business.

It is not always dark.

This letter is emotions overdue
10 But I must let you know
That I call sorrow synonym
For joy confuse pain and pleasure
Nickname love necessity.

So when uncertainties ago the season
15 Was fitful I prayed that He would
Jamaica us, and when fears ago we
Daemocles and Soufriere hung a threat

He did not spill us as I had hoped
So that love could come like a thief
20 And circumstance chisel friendship out of ashes.

II
So burn no holes in your cheek
With tears my friend
The dead are more secure than we
Past the spite in the sun and the farcical smile

25 The habit of living and the dry jest in the
Cracking wind; for earthquakes do not shake
Them though the earth cracks
But we crack at each tumble of the sky.

Resuscitation begins in the dark
30 And out of the night the light is begot;
Eternity is the stretch
And time the boundary stone.
But on the edge of the heart
Wisdom is weak.

35 And I too have paid my bill for sorrow
Cashed my share of tears
Known the currency of the salt cheek
And learnt that grief is no miser.

Daniel Williams
b. ST. VINCENT 1927 d. 1972

The Season of Phantasmal Peace

Then all the nations of birds lifted together
the huge net of the shadows of this earth
in multitudinous dialects, twittering tongues,
stitching and crossing it. They lifted up
5 the shadows of long pines down trackless slopes,
the shadows of glass-faced towers down evening streets,
the shadow of a frail plant on a city sill —
the net rising soundless as night, the birds' cries soundless, until
there was no longer dusk, or season, decline, or weather,
10 only this passage of phantasmal light
that not the narrowest shadow dared to sever.

And men could not see, looking up, what the wild geese drew,
what the ospreys trailed behind them in silvery ropes
that flashed in the icy sunlight; they could not hear
15 battalions of starlings waging peaceful cries,
bearing the net higher, covering this world
like the vines of an orchard, or a mother drawing
the trembling gauze over the trembling eyes
of a child fluttering to sleep;
20   it was the light
that you will see at evening on the side of a hill
in yellow October, and no one hearing knew
what change had brought into the raven's cawing,
the killdeer's screech, the ember-circling chough
25 such an immense, soundless, and high concern
for the fields and cities where the birds belong,
except it was their seasonal passing, Love,
made seasonless, or, from the high privilege of their birth,
something brighter than pity for the wingless ones
35 below them who shared dark holes in windows and in houses,
and higher they lifted the net with soundless voices
above all change, betrayals of falling suns,
and this season lasted one moment, like the pause
between dusk and darkness, between fury and peace,
40 but, for such as our earth is now, it lasted long.

Derek Walcott
b. ST. LUCIA 1930

Day's End

Here in this remote corner,
This neglected fringe of a fishing-village,
Bare with the sea-blast, where only
Cactus flaunt their flagpoles in the sun
5 And the scorched grass seeks precarious tenure
Of the sharp-toothed cliffs of clay,
I saw her one evening: an old woman,
An old peasant woman, barefooted,
Clad in a faded gown, her head
10 Wrapped in a dingy cloth. She walked
Slowly up the hill: her face
Shrivelled with age, skin and bone
Only, the dark living skin
Drawn taut upon the bone that soon
15 Would claim identity with clay and rock.
She walked with regal dignity,
With stark unconscious pride that well
A player-queen might envy,
The dignity that springs from toil and age.
20 Her face, moulded by poverty and resignation,
Hoping for nothing, desiring nothing,
A symbol of this bare and rocky fringe
Carved in a human face, beyond
Either the cares or fears of time.
25 Yet deep within the budding skull
Lingered the tenderness of eyes,
Eyes to reflect the setting sun,
To gaze across the darkening sea
Beyond the memories of her womanhood
30 To spy another lover, death;
The meeting sure. But unafraid,
And proud; proud and regal, unafraid,
A queen waiting to greet her king,
To grasp his hand and go with him
35 Down to her marriage-bed within the earth
Where bone shall bloom to everlastingness.

Frank Collymore
b. BARBADOS 1893 d. 1980

Epitaph

I THINK they will remember this as the age of lamentations,
The age of broken minds and broken souls,
The age of hurt creatures sobbing out their sorrow to the
    rhythm of the blues –
5 The music of lost Africa's desolation become the music of
    the town.

The age of failure of splendid things,
The age of the deformity of splendid things,
The age of old young men and bitter children,
10 The age of treachery and of a great new faith.
The age of madness and machines,
Of broken bodies and fear twisted hearts.

The age of frenzied fumbling and possessive lusts –
And yet, deep down, an age unsatisfied by dirt and guns,
15 An age which though choked by the selfishness of the few
    who owned their bodies and their souls,
Still struggled blindly to the end,
And in their time reached out magnificently
Even for the very stars themselves.

Hugh Doston Carberry
b. JAMAICA 1921

The Knife of Dawn

I make my dance right here!
Right here on the wall of prison I dance.
This world's hope is a blade of fury
and we who are sweepers of an ancient sky
5 discoverers of new planets, sudden stars
we are the world's hope.
And so therefore I rise again I rise again
freedom is a white road with green grass like love.

Out of my time I carve a monument
10 out of a jagged block of convict years I carve it.
The sharp knife of dawn glitters in my hand
but how bare is everything – tall tall tree
infinite air, the unrelaxing tension of the world
and only hope, hope only, the kind eagle soars and
15   wheels in flight.

I dance on the wall of prison
it is not easy to be free and bold
it is not easy to be poised and bound
it is not easy to endure the spike —
20 so river flood, drench not my pillar feet
so river flood, collapse to estuary
only the heart's life, the kind eagle, soars and
    wheels in flight.

Martin Carter
b. GUYANA 1927

PART THREE

Questions on the poems in Part One

Harold Telemaque: In Our Land p. 2

1 Poppies were planted where armies of men died in the 1914–18 European war. What connection is the poet making between cane fields and poppy fields? Why?

2 How do you interpret:
(i) *strike for territory's fences* (19);   (ii) *tint of eye* (24);
(iii) *Sin is not deep* (10).

3 What associations or connotations are connected with ideas of (i) eagles,   (ii) lions,   (iii) blackbirds? What then is the significance of lines 30–32?

4 Discuss:
(i) the effect of repetition in the poem;   (ii) the figurative use of words in the poem;   (iii) the mood, tone, or feeling you sense from the rhythm of the words.

Raymond Barrow: Oh, I Must Hurry p. 3

1 What does the writer call to mind about his country, Belize?

2 The Mayans were one of the ancient peoples of America. What is mentioned about them in the poem?

3 Why does the 'I' think he must hurry? Why would 'regret' (42) be felt?

4 What difference or similarity in tone is there between this poem and *In Our Land* (p. 2)? Give evidence for your view.

Basil McFarlane: Arawak Prologue p. 4

1 What does the phrase, 'the land we have found' (2–3), tell you?

2 What did the person in the poem do 'that bright day' (18)?

3 'Coyaba' was the Arawak word for heaven. What do you make of lines 26–28?

4 What does the narrator tell in the evening? Why do you suppose he is no longer certain it happened?

5 Why does he want to be assured 'at least of the children's respectful silence' (42–43)?

6 What were 'the houses on the water' (29–39) seen by the narrator?

7 'All day we climbed the hill of the sea' (23–25). What is the image being conveyed here?

8 What would you say are the most effective features of this poem?

Edward Brathwaite: Discoverer p. 6

1 'through my summer air' (4). Who does 'my' refer to? What is 'our land' (14)?

2 Whose bones were 'cracked' (21–22)? Who felt 'Pike point, musket butt, and black boot' (19–23)?

3 What dreams and hopes are ascribed to Columbus? What question is asked about those dreams?

4 What do you imagine to be 'the soft voices mocking in the leaves' (32)? What could be 'a return to terrors he had sailed from' (35–36)? What terrors were taking place in Europe at the time? What terrors took place in the lands Columbus discovered?

5 What seems to have been discovered apart from new lands? What, then, is the poet's concern in these lines?

6 Comment on the poet's use of onomatopeia in: (i) line 32;   (ii) 39–40;   (iii) line 3;   (iv) line 38;   (v) line 15; and (vi) line 7.

A. J. Seymour: Carrion Crows p. 7

1 What is carrion? What ideas are usually associated with carrion crows? Are any such ideas used in the poem?

2 What impression of the crows do the following phrases help to convey: 'brooding with evil eyes'; 'feast on swollen carrion'; and 'pestered by flies'?

3 What seems to be the poet's attitude to the crows in the first six lines?

4 The ninth line begins with 'But'. What does this lead you to expect? What impression of the crows does the poet convey in the last six lines? What words and phrases help to give this impression? Is the poet's attitude to the crows a different one now? In what sense, if at all, are the two attitudes consistent with each other?

5 Read the last six lines again. Suppose that instead of these lines the writer had said: 'But I have also seen them flying around and their shadows passing over the fields.' Would that have been as vivid to you? Give your reasons.

Dennis Scott: A Comfort of Crows p. 8

1 How have the birds 'amazed the air' (6)? What 'magnificence' (12) do they make? What are they 'vigilant' (24) about?

2 'Even here' (2, 17). What place is the poet referring to? What is there in lines 17–23 that contrasts with their own magnificence (12) the crows make? What do you imagine 'a new and difficult solace' (26) to be? Which line gives a less romantic aspect of the crows?

3 Do you judge the imagery to be fanciful and contrived or to be fresh and accurate? Support your judgement.

4 Are crows or vultures a common poetic subject or not? Suggest reasons for this. Are they an appropriate subject in this poem? Why or why not? Compare and contrast this poem with *Carrion Crows* (p. 7).

Martin Carter: Till I Collect p. 9

1 What do you imagine to be 'the fence of lights' (2)? Bearing in mind 'shining mud' (1), 'the moon' (1), 'ocean' (2) and 'fence of lights' (2), what do you see as the scene of lines 1–2, 13–14?

2 What do you interpret the 'love' (3) to be? Why would the 'trail' be 'cut by my rudder tempered out of anguish' (5)?

3 What meaning would you give to the line 'to navigate the islands of the stars' (16)?

4 'lest only bones I resurrect to light' (12). What does this line seem to mean? Is it related to 'scattered skeleton' (17)? What do you think, 'skeleton'

represents? Why, do you suppose, does the 'I' wish to collect 'my scattered skeleton'? Can you account for the emphasis on 'till I collect' (17–18)?

Ian McDonald: Yusman Ali, Charcoal Seller p. 10

1 What tragedy befell Yusman Ali?
2 Contrast Yusman Ali's life before and after the tragic incident.
3 The poet has used words that some people still find offensive. Does that spoil the poem?
4 Compare the rhythmic characteristics of the poem with those of *Jaffo the Calypsonian*.

Owen Campbell: The Washerwomen p. 11

1 What do the washerwomen think about while they wash? Why?
2 'Until the shadows come' (48). Which shadows? What do the women do until they come?
3 The poet refers to music more than once. What things does he say make music? How does the poem itself make music?
4 What tone of voice do you hear in lines 33–34? Does it occur elsewhere? Why is it used?
5 What would you suggest as the emotion the poet felt to cause him to write the poem? Use the poem to explain why you think so.

Claude McKay: The Castaways p. 12

1 What kind of scene does the poet evoke in the first seven lines? What does this lead you to expect the poem to be about? At what point do you realise that your expectations will not be met?
2 Who are the Castaways referred to? How does the poet feel about them? What, do you imagine, is meant by 'life's shadows dark and deep'?
3 If the poet's concern is for the 'castaways', are the first seven lines irrelevant? How do they contribute to the poet's effectiveness in drawing attention to the sufferers in the poem?
4 What is the basic contrast being used by the poet, and why does he use it?

5 Are 'vivid grass', 'butterflies', 'sparrows', 'dandelions',
'rare daffodils', and 'thrushes' subjects or objects of
the verb 'behold'? Is this what one would have
expected on reading the first seven lines? What
purpose does the poet's inversion of normal sentence
structure serve? Do you think that poets should invert
normal sentence structures as a general rule? Does
this automatically make lines poetic?

6 Into how many units does the poem divide according
to punctuation? See if each section is concerned with
something particular to itself. How do the sections
relate to each other?

7 What is the concern shared by Louise Bennett in
Dutty Tough and Claude McKay in *The Castaways*? Do
you find one treatment more effective than the other?

A. L. Hendriks: Albert p. 13˙

1 In the Jamaican dialect 'pant' is said for 'pants'. What
other evidence of Jamaican dialect is there in the
poem?

2 Why do you think the poem was written in a dialect?

3 What did Albert get in death that he didn't have in
life?

4 Which of these do you think predominates in the
tone of the poem: (i) sadness;   (ii) humour;
(iii) irony?

Anthony McNeill: Ode To Brother Joe p. 14

1 A 's'liff' (5) is a pipe commonly used for smoking
marijuana, which is illegal in many countries. The
s'liff is used by those members of the Rastafarian sect
who smoke it. Who, then, is Brother Joe? What is
meant by 'his head swollen with certainties' (3–4)?
What are the certainties and who is certain about
them? Who are 'the Babylon' (22) and what is 'the
weed' (40)?

2 What do you think is meant by 'the door to God,
usually shut' (3)? How do you interpret 'a rainbow
gust' (8)? Is it connected with 'furnace of optimism'
(20)?

3 What do you imagine is 'the promised ship' (28)?
What is done with the word 'Freeport' (30)?

4 Who, do you imagine, called Joe 'a martyr' (36)? Why? What difference did it make to the usual activities? Who showed some sorrow? How?

5 What do you think was the intention of the poet in writing the poem? Why do you think so?

Dennis Scott: Squatter's Rites p. 15

1 What do you glean from the poem about the 'facts' in the squatter's life: What did he do? What was his name? What happened to him?

2 What do the words 'king', 'dignity', 'majesty', 'deposition', and 'anarchy' suggest about the second way in which the poet wishes us to see the squatter's life? What does the phrase 'parliament of *dreams*' tell us about this way of seeing the squatter's life? Whose were the dreams?

3 How significant do you think is the difference between the life of the squatter and that of his son? What is the effect of the cliché 'dug' (referring to the son's activity) coming as it does after the description of the old man's kind of digging? Do you find any similarity between the attitudes of father and son to their own activities?

4 What happened 'at night' when the band played 'soul'? What suggestions does the poet build into the last nine lines?

5 Consider the descriptive and emotional value of (i) 'snarled anarchy';   (ii) 'threading the shuddered moths';   (iii) 'leaf-white, senatorial lizards'; (iv) 'leaning in its hole/like a sceptre'. How do these phrases fit into the meaning of the poem?

6 Comment on the suggestions in the title of the poem – to what extent does the poem bear out these suggestions?

Michael Smith: Me Cyaan Believe it p. 17

1 In which West Indian dialect is the poem written? Do you find it easy to understand or not? Does it hinder you from sensing what the poem is about?

2. 'Me a face me reality' (12) What are some of the daily events of that reality?

3 'partisan politricks' (17) is a way of saying partisan
   party politics with a play on the word 'tricks'. What
   perception of the politics of the country does that
   present? What treatment is given to victims (16) in the
   society?

4 'Yuh blind yuh eye to it' (96). To what? To whom is
   the 'I' of the poem talking? What feelings do you
   expect the 'I' to have about the person or persons
   spoken to? Why?

5 To what effect has the poet used repetition in the
   poem?

Anthony McNeill: Ad. for a Housing Scheme p. 20

1 How are the buildings of the housing scheme or
   settlement described?

2 What does the 'I' of the poem find unpleasant about
   his house? What does he seem to be resenting? Do
   you think the people who drive past share his views,
   or does he just see them that way?

3 What picture of the life of the 'I' comes to your mind?
   Why?

Martin Carter: University of Hunger p. 21

1 British Guiana (now Guyana) went through some
   restless times in the early 1950s when the people
   wanted to get rid of British colonial rule. Many people
   died. The poet himself was interned and wrote his
   book *Poems of Resistance* in jail. Who would you
   take to be 'the dark ones/the half sunken in the land'
   (18–19)? Why did they have no voice in 'the
   emptiness/in the unbelievable' (20–21)? What could
   'the shadowless' (22) be?

2 'O Long is the march of men and long is the life' (26,
   47). What does that seem to indicate about the
   'pilgrimage' referred to in line 2? Why is that
   pilgrimage described as 'the university of hunger' (1)?

3 Who do you imagine to be 'the cocks of dawn' (40)?
   What is the dawn the poet sees? Why did the 'cocks
   of dawn' have 'no voice in the emptiness/in the
   unbelievable/in the shadowless' (44)?

4 Which lines speak of women falling into prostitution?
   Which other words, phrases or lines tell what the
   people were marching about?

5 What reason can you see for the use of 'is' for 'it is'?
   Do you find the imagery of the poem easy to visualise
   or not? Say why. To what extent, does the poem rely
   on imagery for its impact?

Edward Brathwaite: *from* The Dust p. 22

1 This, too, is a poem in a dialect. Does that interfere
   with how you approach it? Are your expectations
   coloured by the fact that it is expressed in a dialect?

2 Why are references to youth and strength as well as
   to age and infirmity made? Does the tone of voice
   used to make those references suggest: (i) laughter
   and amusement, or (ii) sneering and jeering, or
   (iii) sadness and regret? Why? What effect does the
   last line of the poem have on you?

3 What organises the language of the poem, apart from
   rhyme, to make it different from loose everyday talk?

Eric Roach: Homestead p. 24

1 What are 'the trades' (1)? What do the cedars do?
   What happens when 'the drought returns' (5)?

2 'And going, left me heritage' (17). What is the heritage?
   Who left it? How did it come into being?

3 What is the third stanza (21–30) telling about? What
   do you understand by the line 'His life was
   unadorned as bread' (23)? What else is said about his
   life? What is 'the fervour' (31) felt about?

4 To whom does 'unsung' (45) refer? What is it implied
   should be sung about? What do you think is meant by
   'And give her substance, give her worth' (50)?

5 Are the persons referred to as nourishers of the
   earth's best blood (59) the same as those who nourish
   arteries of the earth (49)? If not, why is *nourish* used
   in each case? Who are to Reclaim the weary dying
   good (60)? How?

6 'Returns no fragrance . . .' (20). Choose some words,
   phrases, or lines where you find 'fragrance' returned
   and say how memorable you judge each to be and
   why.

7 'my song' (31). Would you agree that the poem has
   characteristics of a song? Give your reason or reasons.

Anthony McNeill: Husks p. 26

1 How soon do you discover that the poem is speaking about birds? When do you know that the birds are vultures or crows? What is the 'undercarriage' (2) referring to? What do you imagine from the phrase 'less vultures than children' (11)?

2 What are steppes? What do you think the poet intended in saying 'our steppes' (15)?

3 How would you explain the following phrases: (i) 'that charming balance disrupts' (17); (ii) 'cropped into dread/fallen angels' (18–19)?

4 What do you take 'husks of the spirit' (25) to mean? Does the poem have any evidence to suggest a death of the spirit? If you think so, think of the way it might have died. If you think the husks are dead but the spirit is surviving, think of what the spirit might have survived from.

Dennis Scott: Bird p. 27

1 What do you imagine the bird doing? Why did the friend say 'Watch this' (19)? Why did the boy's throat grow 'tight with warning' (20)? What do you think caused the friend to tell the boy 'makes your eyes run' (26)? Was it, in your interpretation, the sun that made the boy's eyes run, or something else?

2 Why do you suppose did the poet describe the bird at such length? What do you imagine from line 2? How do you interpret lines 13–14?

3 How authentic, striking, or memorable do you find each of these as images? Say why.
(i) 'in the sly wind way' (3); (ii) 'its mute madrigal' (7); (iii) 'down the slow day' (10); (iv) 'the white round air' (14); (v) 'the steep sky' (17); and (vi) 'the feathered morning' (21)

4 Can you find any examples of the use of any of the following devices in the poem? (i) alliteration; (ii) internal rhyme; (iii) effective repetition.

5 Do you think the poem is sentimental or not? Justify your response.

Dennis Craig: Flowers p. 28

1 What images of 'my world' (2) are presented? What feelings do they arouse?

2 What particular effects do you suppose the writer chose these words to have? (i) 'blanched' (5); (ii) 'cowers' (5); (iii) 'stagnant' (6); (iv) 'thundered' (12)

3 'came stark glory' (11). What brought the glory? What was the glory? Why was it glory? What effect does the 'glory' have on the perception of 'my world' (2)?

4 What emotion do you suppose gave rise to the writing of this poem? Why do you think so?

Mervyn Morris: The Pond p. 28

1 What did the old people say of the pond?

2 'Drawn so hard by prohibitions.' (9) What does this mean? Have you ever been drawn by prohibitions? Give an instance or two.

3 How did the boy get to the pond?

4 Why was the pond dark and mysterious when he got there?

5 We have a strange ending to what appears to be a simple story-poem. Which of these, if any, is the poet telling us in this poem?
(i) imagined fears disappear when faced; (ii) old people frighten children with stories to keep them from danger; (iii) the source of all evil is in ourselves.
Explain why you chose (i), (ii), or (iii), or why you chose none of them.

6 When you read this poem aloud (as you should do all poems over and over) what makes it sound like ordinary conversational speech? What makes it sound different from ordinary conversational speech?

Victor Questel: Pa p. 29

1 What picture do you see of the ageing man?

2 What change of anchorage sums up his predicament?

3 What is there in the poem to indicate love and gratitude?

4 By what means has the poet conveyed the strength of his feeling?

Barbara Ferland: Ave Maria p. 30

1 The Hail Mary or Ave Maria is a prayer recited by the whole congregation. What words of it are quoted in the poem? What does it have to do with the little girl in the poem?

2 What are you told about the little girl and the place?

3 What fruit is offered in the prayer? Is it the same as what is on the trees outside the window? What does the poem pray for for the child with respect to the fruit? Is the poet suggesting that one of the kinds of fruit is of more value to the little black girl? If so, which one?

4 Why should the poet say we must pray 'for the blameless' (20)? Why should the blameless be in need of prayer? How does that view recall the poet's concern in *The Stenographer*?

5 What effect, if any, are you aware of from the writer's interspersing of phrases of the prayer with commentary on the place? If you can find them, read *The Naming of Parts* by Henry Reed and *Exercise Book* by Jacques Prevert and compare them with this poem.

James Berry: Thinking Back on Yard Time p. 31

1 Who, would you say, are the 'we' in the poem? Justify your answer.

2 What do the 'we' do? For what reason?

3 To what extent do you enter into the experience of the poem? What helps you to do that?

4 What do you find to be fresh and new in the poem? Is there anything which you feel is stale and hackneyed in the poem? Give reasons for your answer.

Harold Telemaque: Roots p. 32

1 The stanzas all begin with 'Who'. Do you think questions are being asked or statements being made? Why?

2 What experiences of the 'who' are being recalled in the poem?

3 Why do you suppose the poem was called 'Roots'? In what sense is it like *The Tree* by H. A. Vaughan?

Eric Roach: To My Mother (Versions 1 & 2) p. 33

'To My Mother' exists in several versions. The present
version is based on one which appeared in *Caribbean
Quarterly*, Vol. 5, No. 3, April 1958.

1 In the *Caribbean Quarterly* version line 17 runs
'Hoeing the growing reaping the ripe corn' and line 25
'Praise life's continuity the endless year'. We have
preferred versions of these lines found in manuscripts
now held in the U.W.I. Library, St. Augustine. What
difference do you find between 'Hoeing the ground
reaping the ripe corn' (our version) and 'Hoeing the
growing reaping the ripe corn' (the CQ version)? Look
especially at the '-ing' sounds in the CQ version.

Compare also our version 'Praise life's revival
through the eternal year' with the CQ version 'Praise
life's continuity the endless year'. In addition to
choice of words, consider the position of the line
break in each case and what effect it has on the
words following the break.

2 A manuscript version of stanza three runs as follows:

Come of your middle years, your july loins
I never saw, as in those girls I kissed,
the glory of your beauty in first bloom;
you seemed tenacious as dry season scrub
an iron tool for the stoneland we farmed
to hoe the ground, reap the ripening corn
to knead and thump the thick brown dough for
bread.

(i) What lines are deleted from the manuscript
version?

(ii) Do the deletions improve the poem?

(iii) Compare 'The image of your beauty growing
green' with the line for which it has been
substituted, 'the glory of your beauty in first
bloom'. Which line do you prefer, and why?

(iv) What is the effect of the poet's addition of the line
'Your bone's adolescence I could not know'? What
image or idea does it introduce and how does it
relate to the 'beauty growing green' in the
previous line?

(v) Which works better for you: 'tenacious as dry
season scrub' or 'strong and tough as guava
scrub'? You might like to consider the description
of the mother in the next stanza before you
answer.

H. A. Vaughan: Revelation p. 35

1 Who is being asked to 'turn sideways' (1) What is the 'burnished beauty nearer home' (8)? What are 'dusky limbs' (11)?

2 The words 'the schools' (2) could mean either places with students and teachers or sets of ideas and beliefs called schools of thought. Which do you think they mean? Why?

3 In the 19th century colonising Europeans spread the idea that white Europeans and their civilisation were superior to others. Who do you think are the fools 'who always prate of Greece and Rome' (5)?

4 What would you say makes the poem beautifully lyrical?

Cecil Gray: Caribbean Journal p. 35

1 What is the scene described in the poem?

2 'He stands outside the fencing' (1). What else is he outside of? Why would they 'hear his curse' (13)?

3 Would you say that the poem contains symbols? If so, what are they and what are they symbols of?

4 The poem was originally titled 'Jamaica Journal 1969'. What reason do you suppose caused a change of title?

Shana Yardan: Earth is Brown p. 36

1 'Hannuman' (38) is the Hindu monkey god; a 'tabla' (41) is pair of small drums; 'a sitar' (52) is an instrument like a guitar. What do you suppose 'logie' (39) and 'ghoola' (48) to mean?

2 'For you cannot remember India' (10). What does that and lines 11–16 tell you about the grandfather? Why does his soul now have an 'empty placelessness' (8)? What does he continue to believe and do.

3 What is it the sons do not know and do not want to understand? What seems to be the difference between the sons and their father in their beliefs and way of life? How do you know the grandchild's attitude to the grandfather is different from that of the sons?

4 Why, do you suppose, does the grandchild say ' a dhoti' (loincloth) has become 'a shroud' and 'straight hair a curse' (4–5) in that land?

5 What is the feeling brought out by the poem? Say why you think so.

6 Compare this poem with *Ancestor on the Auction Block* (p. 106) and *The Saddhu of Couva* (p. 38). What similarities and differences do you observe?

Derek Walcott: The Saddhu of Couva p. 38

1 A saddhu or sadhu is a holy man or sage of the Hindu religion. Couva is a village in Trinidad. Some of the older people of East Indian descent in that country look back to India as home. Who is the 'I' speaking in the poem? What is the first clue you get about his dialect? What do you understand him to mean by 'for my spirit, India is too far' (8)? Why does he call certain things 'sacred' (11,12, 23, 35)? With what ideas are 'the gods' (47) associated? What do lines 47–54 tell you about his beliefs? How do you then imagine he feels about India? The 'Ramayana' (21) is the Hindu sacred epic or story, written about 300 BC, in which the hero, Rama, struggles against evil and is helped by the 'monkey' general or god, Hanuman. Why does the 'I' refer to it?

2 'Uttar Pradesh' (25) and 'West Bengal' (24) are states in India. What do you think 'Ramlochan Repairs' (25) means? Why, do you suppose, does the 'I' say 'even to Ramlochan' (12)? How does he seem to regard 'Indian hits' (13) and Ramlochan? How could Uttar Pradesh be behind Ramlochan Repairs (25)? Where do you take the ancient temples (24) to be? Why, do you imagine, does the 'I' say 'Once' (22)? What reason did the 'I' give when he said I did not miss them (24)? What seems to be 'their sacred language' (35) now?

3 Who would you take an Elder to be? What do you understand from 'Playing the Elder' (43)? In what way or ways do you imagine he played the Elder? Why do you think he says 'There are no more Elders,/Is only old people' (43–44)? What is the change he is looking at? How does he seem to feel about it? What does he consider as an explanation in lines 46–54?

4 Cremation is the burning of a corpse. What does 'its cremation' (58) refer to? 'Sandalwood' (59) is used when the body of an important person of the Hindu religion is cremated. What 'bed' (59) does the 'I' speak of? What do you imagine makes him think of it? What significance would you give to the word 'ascend' (59)? What part does the image of 'white bird' (30) play in the poem?

5 'Mantras' (16) are hymns; 'a sitar' (17) is a musical
 instrument resembling a guitar; 'Divali' (18) is the
 Hindu festival of lights; 'Anopheles' (17) is the name of
 a type of mosquito. Comment on the comparisons
 made in lines 16–18. Comment on any other similes
 and metaphors you find striking or memorable or
 unusual.

6 Compare and contrast this poem with *Earth is Brown*
 (p. 36).

Edward Brathwaite: Tizzic p. 40

1 What country is indicated by 'calypso-season camp'
 (7), 'the jump-up' (3), and 'road-march tramp' (8)?
 What 'blazed for two nights' (14) there? What
 happened to Tizzic then?

2 'Kitch', 'Sparrow' and 'Dougla' are names of
 Trinidadian calypsonians. Why are they mentioned?
 What do you think is meant by 'his heightened,
 borrowed glory' (16–17)? How important was that to
 Tizzic? How do you interpret 'saved him' (3–4)?

3 'his have-nothing cottage' (5–6). What does that and
 'holes, damp, rain through the roof' tell about Tizzic?
 When could he 'no longer feel the cramp of poverty's
 confinement, spirit's damp' (23–24)? What is the
 significance of lines 33–34?

4 Why is the use of rhyme so important in this poem?
 Is the reason related to 'their little working songs' (11)
 in any way?

5 How extensive is the use of metaphor? Would you
 expect metaphor to be used extensively to reflect the
 Trinidad Carnival or not? Give reasons.

6 Compare the theme and treatment in this poem with
 those in *Jaffo the Calypsoniän* (p. 69) and *Mass Man*
 (p. 74).

Cecil Herbert: Lines Written on a Train p. 41

1 What do you think the poet is describing as 'the
 spirituals the peasants sing' (3) and 'the choirs/That
 moving sing and singing reap/The canes' (11–13)?

2 Cane fires sometimes spread too quickly. What did
 the 'I' see that time? Where is the person who is
 seeing?

3 What does the narrator of the poem think about the
 peasants as they work?

4 What is it that 'He would not understand who sits at my side' (6–7)? What happens to cause 'my eyes to fill with tears' (5)?

5 A river of some kind soothes the hurts and pain of the peasants' lives (16). Why should the poet be 'afraid' (19) of such soothing? What 'fire' (20) would such a river absorb? How does that relate to line 14 of *Poem* by the same poet?

6 Do you find any evidence of onomatopeia in the poem?

7 What lines or phrases do you find especially lyrical?

E. McG. Keane: Country p. 42

1 What is suggested about the people in the new country in lines 1–6?

2 What is suggested about other people in lines 7–13?

3 What do you understand by 'persecute you with pen and ink' (11)? Why should people who have 'found out about things' (13) be 'sad' (12)?

4 In what sense is the word 'crude' (15) used? Is crude oil similar in any way to 'the crude country' (15)?

5 What do you think motivated the poet to write this poem?

John Agard: Limbo Dancer at Immigration p. 43

1 Is the person called a limbo dancer because he or she is a limbo dancer or for some other reason? If for some other reason, what do you think it is? Why does he/she say he/she always gets 'the same hassle from authorities' (5–6)?

2 Why does the person refer to 'slaveship' (13, 20), 'lynchings' (33), ' chains' (36)? How does the reference to 'nails' (30) fit in?

3 What do you see as the significance of lines 38–41?

4 What do you think accounts for the strong impact the poem has?

H. A. Vaughan: In Absence p. 45

1 What are the things that she must not know? Why is she not to know?

2 What does the final line of the poem convey to you? Is that referred to elsewhere?

3 What would you say gives this poem its appeal as a love poem?

Mervyn Morris: Family Pictures p. 46

1 What pictures of family life are presented in the poem? Who is the 'him' (3)? What does the 'wife' (13) do? What does the 'him' think that his family feel for him?

2 'it is a private sanctuary' (27). What is? What goes on in it? How does the 'him' feel about that?

3 'this dream' (37). Would you agree that the dream is to go to the beach? If no, then what is the dream? Why is the word 'cage' (45) used? What do you suppose prompts the dream?

4 Comment on the use of each of the following in the poem: (i) metaphor; (ii) rhyme; (iii) rhythm; (iv) dramatic irony.

5 Compare this poem with *A Family Man* (p. 147) with respect to the concerns of the two poets.

Mervyn Morris: Birthday Honours p. 47

1 Whose birthday is referred to? What makes you think so?

2 The poet John Donne is mentioned in line 6. What is said about him in lines 6–11? Why does the poet say in line 12 'Love is a theme for prose'? What does he have in mind in saying: (a) 'love in art is lies' (37); (b) 'Good lies may testify of love' (14)?

3 'Let me shape a poem' (13). How does the poet show what his shaping of a poem involved? What connections, if any, do the quotation marks used between lines 16 and 24 have with lines 13–14? What is the 'something I can do' (41)?

4 What do you see as the poet's reason or reasons for saying what he does in lines 25–26? What importance do the things mentioned in lines 30–31 have? What are they markers of? What do you think is meant by 'all our times are one' (34)?

5 What evidence, if any, is there in the poem of: (i) paradox; (ii) irony?

E. A. Markham: Philpot Puzzled p. 49

1 What does she mean by 'someone else' (1)? What is 'his new status' (16)? Who was 'Roy' (11)?

2 What difference took place in Maureen's language and manner? What is Philpot puzzled about?

3 What resemblances and differences are there in *Philpot Puzzled* and *In Absence*?

Derek Walcott: Anna p. 50

1 This is an excerpt from *Another Life*. Who is 'Still dreamt of, still missed' (1)? What clues tell you when the narrator knew Anna? How could you interpret line 34?

2 What picture of Anna does the 'I' still see in his mind? What memories of past events? Who accused whom of a grave deep wrong (9) and wound (9) inflicted on Anna? What do you suppose the wrong was? What 'goodbyes' (42) do you think Anna endured?

3 The other Annas – Anna Karenina and Anna Christic – are characters in foreign novels. What do you imagine is meant by 'I found life within some novel's leaves more real than you ' (45–46)? How, then, do you suppose the Anna of this poem became ' another country' (26)? Why was she, like the other Annas, 'his doomed heroine' (47)? What influence did the world of novels and literature have on the 'I'? 'You knew, you knew' (47). Knew what?

4 What does the poem contain from the world of 'some novel's leaves' (45)? What do you think is referred to as 'our brassy season' (15)? The narrator says it is 'our imitation autumn' instead of regarding autumn as an imitation of our brassy season. Does that reveal anything of his attitude to foreign places and people? Would you describe the narrator as any of these: cruel, grateful, hypocritical, saddened, nostalgic, cynical, regretful, sentimental? Give reasons for your answers.

5 What comparisons in the poem do you find most striking and memorable? Comment on the poet's imagination.

Anthony McNeill: Notes on a September Day p. 52

1 There are nightingales in Jamaica. What happened to this particular 'nightingale' (1)? What does 'death-pinned' (2–3) tell you? What did he do before? What is happening now where the nightingale sang before?

2 The 'otaheite' (5) is a fruit. In Jamaica it is called the otaheite apple, in Trinidad and other places the 'pomme arac' or 'pommearac'. It is red and shaped like an avocado pear, but smaller. In which two lines does the poet describe it? Do you see any reason why certain associations are aroused in those lines? What do you understand by 'the lean season' (11)?

3 Why, do you suppose, is the person's body described as 'seasonal' (26)? What is the 'rigor mortis' (27) (i.e. death) that stiffens it? Is it the same as the nightingale's?

4 Which of these emotions would you say the poem is expressing: (i) ecstasy; (ii) anger; (iii) regret; (iv) amusement. What causes the particular emotion?

Wayne Brown: Drought p. 53

1 'The woman is barren' (1, 4). In what tone of voice do you hear this line? Why? What pictures of aridness, desolation and emptiness does the poem present? Why?

2 What does the song or cry of the woman convey to you? What is she looking for with hope? Why does the poet direct her appeal to the whole world? How do you interpret 'ploughed crater' (14)?

3 'The city . . . will soon be around her ankles' (6). What meaning would you give to this line? Why? What is conveyed by 'crawling south like an oil slick' (5)?

4 'The woman . . . dances palely each evening/Among the fallen blackbirds' (16–17). What does 'palely' tell you about the woman? Why blackbirds? Why does she dance among them? Why are they said to be fallen? How does 'sunset of her time' (14) fit with her dancing?

5 Discuss the poem with respect to the following themes: compassion, scorn, understanding, anger, pity and mockery.

Cheryl Albury: Poem for Mothers p. 54

1 What picture of men-women relationships does the poem give?

2 In what way was the 'I' of the poem a victim?

3 What feeling caused the poem to be written? Does it give a fair or balanced picture of men-women relationships in spite of that feeling, or not?

Cheryl Albury: Superwife p. 55

1 What chores of a housewife are referred to? Why?
2 Why does the poet describe the 'her' as a programmed idiot?
3 What fate does the poem suggest awaits housewives?
4 Do you think the poet is a housewife or not? Say why.

Dionne Brand: Old I and Old II p. 56

1 What do you think are 'flour bag drawers' (3) and 'stretch marked legs' (4)?
2 What might be the shabby secrets (7) to be told?
3 Compare Old I with Old II with respect to (i) mood and (ii) imagery.

Pamela Mordecai: Tell Me p. 57

1 How do you interpret 'I'm well fixed for all love's traffic' (6–7)? Why? What else does the 'I' offer?
2 What do you think is meant by 'I know it sounds a little much' (22–23)?
3 Who is being asked 'what have you got to give' (26)? Why?

Judy Miles: Summer and Kitsilano Beach p. 58

1 What do you think is being described as 'the rotting heads/vomited by the retreating tides' (2–3)?
2 At the very beginning what do the words 'rotting' (2) and 'vomited' (3) suggest about the mood and attitude to be found in the poem?
3 What is suggested that the dark haired girl might do? Why is her way of sitting remarked upon? What seems to be the attitude of the poet to the girl?
4 Why is the man described as 'looking from the corners of his pointed eyes' (15–16)? Why are the words 'writhing' (18) and 'lust' (29) used? Is there an assonant echo associated with 'tentacles' (20)?
5 For whom is your sympathy or pity aroused, the dark haired girl, the man, or the narrator of the poem?

Judy Miles: Lunch Hour p. 59

1 What is the setting for the poem? Say why you think
so.

2 Who serves 'aloofness' (9)? What is meant by
'Waiting/bites hugely/into the time' (10–13)? Why, do
you suppose, is the waiter's smile described as an
'instant coffee smile' (15)? Why, do you imagine, is the
atmosphere described as 'formica' (6)?

3 What do you think is meant by saying the 'young girl
barricades/herself behind a stare/as hard as toast'
(23–26)? What is she afraid of? Why, then, does she go
to the 'romantic alcove' (19)? Why, in your
understanding, does she imagine 'passions
discarded/like cheap coats' (29–30)?

4 Would you say there is any sadness in this poem, or
not? Say why.

Christine Craig: Crow Poem p. 60

1 What does the 'I' think she is unable to do? How does
she regard her efforts? What is she convinced of?

2 Why, do you suppose, did the poet choose a crow to
make the comparison in the poem?

3 What is the irony expressed in the last three lines of
the poem?

Patrick Rahming: Mailboat to Hell p. 61

1 The *status quo* means the way things are at present.
Who would you say are the souls cursing 'John Statusquo' (6) and crying 'Freedom and Justice' (5)?

2 What do you think the 'I' is referring to as the
'mailboat to hell'? How would you interpret:
(i) 'ship' (11); (ii) 'captain' (12); (iii) 'crew' (12),
(iv) 'the crowd' (13); (v) 'the few' (14)?

3 What is the feeling communicated by the poem?
About what?

Martin Carter: This is The Dark Time, My Love p. 62

1 'Everywhere the faces of men are strained and
anxious' (8). What do you think this information has
to do with 'boot of steel' (10), 'man of death' (11), and
'the stranger invader' (11)?

2 The poet is a Guyanese. Is there anything in the poem to suggest that he is telling of the time (1953) when the freedom of British Guiana (as Guyana was then) was suspended and British soldiers controlled the country because it was said that communism would take over? Who or what could the 'Red flowers' (4) be? What would you take 'your dream' (12) to mean?

3 How well does the description the 'dark time' (1) fit the poem? What events made it a dark time? How do you interpret 'The shining sun is hidden in the sky' (3)? Who or what, do you think, are 'brown beetles' (2), 'dark metal' (6) and 'the slender grass' (10)?

4 What feeling is conveyed with 'watching you sleep' (12)? What effect or force does the poem as a whole have on you? Can you suggest why?

Gloria Escoffery: No Man's Land p. 63

1 Political violence has sometimes erupted in the writer's country. What is described in lines 1–7?

2 What do you take 'caught playing politics' (1) to mean? Why the bracketed question mark in line 5?

3 What is described in lines 8–11?

4 'baby mother' (8) is used to mean baby's mother, mother of someone's baby. Who do you think are the 'baby mother' (8) and 'the matron' (11)? How does each one behave?

5 In what sense do you take 'forever' (9) in relation to the photographer and the morning paper?

6 What is the word 'traditional' (10) used to suggest?

7 There is a famous sculpture by Michelangelo in the Vatican in Rome called 'Pieta'. It depicts the mother of Christ holding the body of her crucified son across her lap and the pity and sorrow she felt. What does the poet mean there by 'this pieta' (15)?

8 Bearing in mind what things are kept in a museum, why do you suppose the writer says this 'pieta . . . belongs within the pietas of a museum frame' (15–17)? What is the full significance of the question of line 18?

Mervyn Morris: To the Unknown Non-Combatant p. 64

1 A non-combatant is a person who during a war is not himself engaged in that war. Why was the 'he' of the poem 'in the open street' (3)?

2 How would you explain 'voices from the left' (5) and 'voices from the right' (8)?

3 Why do you think 'he' was told 'be honest with yourself, you're ours' (7)?

4 'Come help us in the fight' (6). What fight? Why do you suppose he thought perhaps he'd better choose (13)?

5 Why do you think 'he' was left in the dust, forgotten? What is the poet pointing to?

Ian McDonald: A White Man Considers the Situation p. 65

1 'My brutal tenancy' (5). Where do you think that 'tenancy' took place? Whose 'tenancy' is meant? Why is it being regarded as a tenancy? Who do you think called it brutal? Why?

2 Do you think the 'I' of the poem is guilty of brutal tenancy? Say why or why not. How does he seem to feel about his 'dark-skinned love' (21)? Why does he say 'the best measure is the use of time' (15, 20)?

3 What changes seem to be taking place in the land? Who seem to be the black sentries (28)?

4 Why does the 'I' lie 'sleepless' (25)?

5 What use has the poet made of symbols?

6 What is the feeling at the end of the poem? What is the effect of the repetition in line 30?

Derek Walcott: Parades, Parades p. 66

1 Why is a 'white cork-hat' (17) being worn? What do the children in 'the uniforms of the country' (22–23) have to do with it? In relation to that occasion what do you think is meant by 'when the law lived far away' (28)? Who do you suppose is called 'the fool' (16)?

2 'so the politicians plod without imagination' (8–9). Why do you suppose, has the 'I' repeated 'old' (2, 14) and used 'same' (6, 10, 14, 15) four times? What do you gather the 'I' is saying about the politicians of the day? What does he seem to think might have been better? Which lines are used to suggest that?

3 Who, do you imagine, is being ridiculed in lines 34–37? What happens when the person appears? Is any reason given why 'the silence' (41) is not to be

taken as 'respect' (42)? From whose point of view are the children seen as 'bewildered and shy' (24)? How does the 'I' seem to interpret that look on the faces of the electorate (46–47)? What does he seem to mean by 'how it all happened' (48)?

4 Is there any evidence in the poem to bear out that the 'I' is an imperialist or merely a supporter of an opposition party? If not, is he just denigrating West Indian elected leaders in order to appear to be an intellectual, as many West Indians now do, or can you find evidence of some other motive?

5 Compare and contrast this poem and *O Dreams, O Destinations* (p. 67)

6. Compare the fear in *Lines Written on a Train* (p. 41) with the doubt and pain in this poem.

Edward Brathwaite: O Dreams O Destinations p. 67

1 In a famous short story, *The Secret Life of Walter Mitty*, James Thurber tells how Walter Mitty used to go off into fantasies in which he was always a daring hero. What is the poem saying in 'each in his Walter Mitty world a wild Napoleon' (16–17)? What assessment does the poem place on 'our islands' leaders' (12)? What is implied in 'anxious that their single-minded fames should rise' (21–22)?

2 'still on the floor with soldiers' (10–11). What do children do on the floor with toy soldiers? With what is the poem connecting such child's play? Why?

3 What do you suppose is 'the selfishness no longer young' (9–10)?

4 Why are the poor called 'the supporting poor' (25)? What does the poem say happens to them? Do you find anything offensive there or not?

5 Which ones of these would you say the poem is concerned with: (i) pleasant fantasies; (ii) arrogance and corruption; (iii) defence of democracy; (iv) betrayal of the poor; (v) lost dreams? Give reasons for your answer.

6 Would you say the poem denigrates or merely criticises our islands' leaders? What do you imagine could be the result if people were encouraged merely to denigrate leaders? How does that serve the interests of imperialists? Does the poet seem to support imperialism?

Ian McDonald: Jaffo the Calypsonian p. 69

1 Enumerate all the 'facts' of Jaffo's life given in the poem. What force do these 'facts' have on you?

2 Do you think the poet was more interested in awakening your sympathy for Jaffo or in giving you a realisation of the strength of Jaffo's obsession? Argue the matter with quotations from the poem.

3 What kind of image and feeling do you get from each of these?
   (i) ragged still-eyed men;   (ii) the look of unsung calypsoes stared in his eyes;   (iii) rat-trap rum shops;   (iv) respectable eyes.

4 The poet puts certain phrases together for the kind of sounds the words have, as well as for other reasons. What effects or suggestions do you hear from the sounds in these phrases?
   (i) clogged throat;   (ii) sang and sang with staccato shout;   (iii) thickened to a hard final silence;   (iv) grated in brassy fear.

5 Can you detect the beat and rhythm of the poet's language in this poem? Does it have any resemblance or relation to the subject matter of the poem? If so, explain the relationship. Does it fit or contrast with Jaffo's fate? What reason could the poet have had for using it?

Vivian Virtue: Landscape Painter, Jamaica p. 71

1 Who is being watched in the poem? Why, do you suppose, is the watcher so interested in what the person being watched is doing? Is the watcher being appreciative or critical?

2 Why, do you think, does the writer use the word 'fidgeting' (25) about the little hills? What has that to do with 'frustrating' (27)? What implication for the painter's achievement does that have?

3 What poetic devices are being used in: (i) lines 7–8; and (ii) lines 9–10?

Frank Collymore: Apologia p. 72

1 Which poets are described as 'abortive poets' (1)?

2 What purpose is served by the use of these words in the poem: – 'unknown' (1), 'futility' (3), 'oblivion' (6), 'sandcastles' (7)?

3 What do you take 'the rose that flames upon the vision' (14–15) to mean? How do the 'we' 'pour Out the heart's libation' (10–11)? What is the wine' (12)?

4 To what extent are the comparisons fresh and memorable?

Derek Walcott: For Harry Simmons p. 72

1 This is an excerpt from a book-length poem, *Another Life*, in which the poet tells of his early life in St Lucia, where he was born and where he grew up. Harry Simmons was an artist he knew. What do you find memorable in the description of his physical appearance in lines 1–9?

2 When, do you think, did the people referred to have 'tribal names' (18)? An adze is a tool for cutting or shaping wood; a mattock is like a pick-axe with one edge like an adze; a midden is a heap of refuse or of prehistoric bones and shells. What do they seem to do with 'returned their tribal names' (18)?

3 'and he is a man no more' (25). How do you interpret that line in relation to lines 26 and 27? How are lines 26–27 related to lines 13–17? In what sense is meant 'they had built him themselves' (12)?

John Robert Lee: Vocation p. 73

1 A 'soutane' is a priest's gown. Who do you suppose is referred to as 'you' in line 7?

2 'despite all that' (6). Despite what? Whose hands are clasped 'in fervent unbelief' (2)? Who has 'the stale, old lady's scent of righteousness' (3–4)?

3 What does the poet describe of the country and its people in lines 9–15? What attitude is obliquely expressed?

4 What do you suppose is the 'this' of line 7? Is there a connection between the 'this' of line 7 and what is mentioned in lines 9–15?

5 Who do you suppose has that 'vision waiting gently' (20)? Who would you say 'calm clean pools below the waterfall' (21) symbolises? Is that related to the life of a priest or not?

6 What does the 'I' of the poem mean by 'a common celibacy' (23) to be endured? How is the creation of the 'I' of the poem described? Why is the word 'too' used in line 27?

7 'changing them into some clarity' (31–32). What do
you think is the clarity referred to here? How does
that claim illuminate what is seen as a common
pursuit?

Derek Walcott: Mass Man p. 74

1 In what way do you imagine the clerk 'entered a lion'
(7–8)? What is the first clue in the poem that tells
you? Why, then, are 'peacock' (3) and 'Cleopatra' (10)
mentioned? What do you see is being described as
'that whirlwind's radiance' (12)? When does it take
place?

2 What are the 'they' (11) doing? What are referred to as
'metaphors' (5)? Why? What attitude of the 'I' comes
out with 'coruscating, mincing' (6)?

3 What do you understand by 'a child, rigged as a bat'
(13)? Do you sense a tone of disapproval from the
word 'rigged'? When the 'I' says that he is dancing
too, does he mean dance as in line 11? A 'gibbet' (14)
is a gallows used for hanging people. What do you
take it that the 'I' means in line 15? How, then, does
the 'I' seem to regard the 'they' (11)?

4 What day, do you think, is referred to as 'penitential
morning' (18)? What do ashes have to do with it?
What do you interpret the 'I' to be saying to the 'they'
(11) in lines 19–21? What does the 'I' seem to see as
his role? How does he seem to regard it in relation to
what they are doing?

5 Compare and contrast this poem with *Tizzic* (p. 40).

Roger McTair: Corners Without Answers p. 76

1 What do the 'we' (1) spend hour after hour doing?
Who could be the 'they' (1) that wonder? What do the
'we' do 'Night after night' (12)?

2 Why do they 'form a crowd' (29) and need 'noise'
(31)? Why do you suppose they feel themselves to be
'drifting souls' (32)?

3 What is it that their 'skeptic thoughts refuse belief'
(18)? What could be meant by: (i) the road behind
(10); (ii) the road beyond (9); (iii) the fear within
our hearts (8)?

4 What did the poet intend to express in this poem,
and how did his choice of images help to express it?

A. L. Hendriks: Will the Real Me Please Stand Up? p. 77

1 Do you suppose there is something behind the idea of putting on others' clothes?

2 What do you take each of these to be saying: (i) 'but it smelled of pain' (3); (ii) 'Animals seemed simply suited' (16); (iii) 'something kinetic being needed' (24); (iv) or Leda's bestialism' (29)?

3 Which of these, do you think, could best be described as the theme of the poem: (i) 'playfulness and imagination'; (ii) 'facing the world'; (iii) 'clothes and disguises'?

4 Taking into account the frivolous tone and the adolescent diction of the poem, do you see it as a serious poem or one that is merely amusing? How would you account for any element of contrast used in the poem?

5 Why is 'i' written with a small letter, instead of a capital? Is that just a gimmick or does it have some significance? How would you explain the almost total absence of punctuation?

Heather Royes: Theophilus Jones Walks Naked Down King Street p. 79

1 What do you imagine about 'Theophilus Jones' from 'asphalt-black rag-tag pants' (3–4)? What then was his status in the society in which he lived?

2 Why was his walk described as 'his triumphant march' (7)? What do you think was his motive and intention? Why? What reason can you think of why 'he had wanted to do this for a long time' (10–11)? Was he a madman, as the carwash boys shouted?

3 While Theophilus was making his triumphant march what did it mean to people he did it to defy? What contrasts of indifference seem to mock his gesture? Consider 'Down on the Ferry Pier' (16), 'the sun' (2) 'a plane' (26), and 'the kingfisher' (41). What indifference is to be connected with his 'asphalt-black, rag-tag pants' (3)?

4 Look closely at lines 30–35. In which way is a solemn ritual sacrifice suggested? Theophilus releases himself from degradation. Does his suicide also bring him ennoblement or redemption of character?

5 Bearing in mind the information given in lines 6–18
  was the walk a triumph or a failure? Was it a triumph
  Theophilus had over himself, or was it another of the
  failures of his life? What is the irony in this denial of
  even such a success?

6 What significance would you give lines 37–39 in
  relation to the importance of Theophilus in the
  society?

7 What tragic ironies seem to permeate the poem?
  What comment on society does it convey?

Kendel Hippolyte: Choice of Corpses p. 81

1 Why is the man referred to as 'just a man in sweaty
  khaki' (12)?

2 What relationship do you see between a revolutionary
  'hiding in your room' (4) and 'a revolutionary inside
  your head' (33–34)?

3 What do you take to be the 'choice of corpses' (41)
  referred to?

4 How do lines 31–39 affect you after reading lines
  1–30?

5 How is drama introduced into the poem?

6 In what ways does the poem differ from ordinary
  loose talk?

Marc Matthews: Portia Faces Life p. 82

1 There used to be a soap opera on radio called 'Portia
  Faces Life'. How do you know the 'e' (he) of the poem
  was familiar with it?

2 What events in the life of the 'e' of the poem tell you
  the kind of life he has to face?

3 What picture do you get of the people in the soap
  opera in lines 30–33? What irony is the poem
  expressing in 'all de while/Portia saying/is life she
  facing' (16–18)?

4 What is highlighted by the line 'like nutten is de
  matter' (49)? What is expressed in: (i) 'a bucket of
  newspapers' (13);   (ii) 'cars play jump-in' (14);   (iii)
  'where the dead livin' (15)?

Wayne Brown: Noah p. 84

1 The story about Noah has inspired poems by many poets. What was promised to Noah in that story? Does this poem tell the usual story of Noah and the Ark? Give reasons for your answer.

2 Which words, phrases, and lines show the poet's skill in communicating the imagined experience of being in the ark?

3 'Something, he thought, might come of this' (24–25) ... 'Some good, some Truth' (27). What truth did Noah seem to be hoping for? 'Birth was not the answer,/Nor Death' (31–32). To what? What is presented as Noah's obsession? Was his hope related in any way to 'instinctual, half-lit lives' (26) or not?

4 'Till one day laden with lies,/It brought back promise of fruit, of/Resolution and change' (47–49). What does that tell you about the answer Noah received? What connection does it have with 'Nothing had changed' (57) and 'To where all rainbows/Drown among waves' (67–68)?

5 In what sense could Noah be said to be a representative figure? How common is the disillusionment that the ark of his mind sees?

Derek Walcott: Adios, Carenage p. 86

1 The poem is a part of a longer poem called *The Schooner Flight*. 'Shabine' (17) is a Trinidadian dialect word that used to be used to name a person with African features and hair but of a reddish brown or yellowish complexion; bohbohl (31) or bobol is a Trinidadian word for fraud in business and government. What does the name of the 'I' of the poem tell you? Why do you think he says 'I'm just a red nigger' (40)? What work does he do? How soon do you know that he is speaking a West Indian dialect? What does he seem to mean by 'my common language' (75)? What features of that language might be objectionable to some people? To whom does he refer as the woman I left (21)? What is the Flight (56)?

2 Who was the 'man exactly like me' (23)? What do you understand by the phrase 'the man was weeping' (23)? What was he weeping about? What reason or reasons do you think the poet had for saying 'But they had started to poison my soul' (30)? What do you imagine the poet means by 'when these slums of

empire was paradise' (39)? In what two different
senses would you read the phrase 'go be soaked in
salt' (72)? What seems to you to be the significance of
Flight as the name of the ship?

3 Shabine speaks of writing a poem (71–72). Is there
anything to lead you to expect this seaman to be a
poet? Would you agree that Shabine seems to be
representing the poet who wrote the poem? If so,
what would the leaving seem to mean?

4 What are you made to imagine in the following lines:
(i) 6–10;   (ii) 19–21;   (iii) 45–48;   (iv) 63–64?

Wordsworth A. McAndrew: Ol' Higue p. 89

1 A still-common superstitious belief is that some
women, called old higues or soucouyants, can shed
their skins and fly like a ball of fire to suck the blood
of sleeping victims, but, having to return to their skins
before dawn, may be delayed and caught if salt or rice
is thrown in their way. What happened to the one in
this poem?

2 How does the rhythm used by the poet seem
appropriate to the subject matter of the poem?

Lorna Goodison: Sister Mary and the Devil p. 91

1 What happened to Sister Mary when she saw her
'shadow double' (13)?

2 'fire catch in mi body' (31). What do you think the 'fire'
was? Why do you think she felt ashamed and hid her
face when she felt it?

3 What, do you imagine, made her think of the man as
the devil? Why would a person like Sister Mary blame
a devil for something he or she felt ashamed of?

4 What do you understand by the two lines: (i) 'Today
is Mine Sister Mary' (42):   (ii) 'Sister Mary died' (36)?

5 Comment on the aptness or otherwise of: (i) them
curl up like them want to/sleep (5–6);   (ii) the dust
was powdering/mi clean white shoes (10–11);
(iii) heavy down mi step (18);   (iv) the ground
leave/mi foot (19–20).

Anson Gonzales: Tabiz p. 93

1 The word tabiz (or tabis) is or was used in Trinidad
   and might have come from the French word *tebiser*,
   to give a watered down appearance, in this case to
   evil. Some superstitious beliefs persist in the
   Caribbean. One in Trinidad is that envy, the evil eye,
   or maljo, can bring misfortune; another, that douens
   are ghosts of children who died before baptism; and
   another, that soucouyants are women who shed their
   skins and fly around sucking the blood of persons
   sleeping at night. People who believe such ideas often
   seek a charm or tabiz to protect them. What do you
   think of the idea of a poem being a protective charm
   (i.e. 1–7)?

2 With what different objects does the poet compare
   the poem?

3 What blessings or events of good fortune are
   promised? (Mt Everest is the highest peak in the
   world; El Tucuche is the highest in Trinidad.)

4 What do you think is 'the greater glory' (34) to be
   brought in for assistance?

5 Comment on the language used in the poem and its
   effectiveness.

Dennis Scott: Guard-ring p. 94

1 For the person in the poem what power do the rings
   have? What other power is also believed in?

2 What is there in the poem that suggests what
   happens in some religious services?

3 'I praising yu candle also' (28). Why does the
   supplicant in the poem give this assurance?

4 In what sense is the person in the poem playing it
   safe?

5 'learn me' (25) is used in the Jamaican dialect to mean
   'teach me'. What does the person in the poem wish to
   be taught?

6 What kind of life do you imagine the person leads?

7 Which of the following messages does the poet wish
   to communicate: (i) mockery of the contradictions
   in the person's belief;   (ii) understanding of the
   person's situation;   (iii) disgust with superstitious
   ideas? Give reasons for your answer.

Dennis Scott: Uncle Time p. 96

1 Whom or what do you take to be 'Uncle Time'? Why is he said to be 'cunnin' (cunning) (7)? Why does he 'smile black as sorrow' (11)?

2 How would you explain lines 14–16? What do you understand from lines 17–18?

3 What would you say, then, is the theme of the poem? Why do you think so? Does the poem treat the theme frivolously or seriously? Why do you say so?

4 Which phrases or lines do you find most memorable as images in the poem? Give reasons for your responses.

5 People in the West Indies often expect to be amused or offended by a West Indian dialect. What is the tone of the dialect in this poem?

Edward Brathwaite: So Long, Charlie Parker p. 96

1 Charlie Parker achieved fame as a black American musician in the 1940s. He was sometimes called 'The Bird'. What do the words 'played his heart out' (2–3) make you think of? What impression do the lines 'he wished to hold the night from burning/all time long' (10–11) give you?

2 What is it that the poet suggests that Parker regretted? What suggests that he was expecting death? How is the coming of death described? What is the feeling about Parker that the poem is communicating?

3 What effect, if any, are you aware of from the use of the words 'slowed', 'shivered', 'stopped' and 'slipped' in lines 17–23?

4 Comment on how each of the following help to make the poem memorable: (i) its theme; (ii) its rhythm; (iii) its imagery.

5 Compare this poem, in any way you wish, with *Trane* (p. 173)

Anthony McNeill: Don p. 98

1 Don was a Jamaican musician of the 1960s. What do you see as the reason why the poem is preceded by a quotation? How would you interpret 'heaviest spirit' in the quotation?

2 What comes to mind with the use of the words
'dread' (3), 'sufferer's' (4), 'lock-conscious' (13), and
'Babylon' (14)? What does that seem to have to do
with 'hurt' (1)?

3 'captured you nightly' (2). What do you think 'nightly'
has to do with a musician, like Don? Why, do you
suppose, are 'jukeboxes' mentioned? What does the
phrase 'broken music' (6) suggest to you?

4 The poem begins in standard English, but lines 9–16
suggest another voice. Whose? How can you tell how
that voice regards Don? What is echoed in lines
11–14? What is hoped for in lines 15–16? How does
the first voice regard Don in lines 1–3? What is the
poem as a whole saying about Don?

5 Compare and contrast *Don* with *Trane* (p. 173).

H. A. Vaughan: The Tree p. 99

1 What relationship does the 'I' want with his land or
country? Why does he want his roots to 'go deep' (5)?

2 Why does he wish for golden words (16)? How do you
suppose he wishes to 'spread essential joys/For the
world's release' (19–20)?

3 What do you suppose gives the poem its strength of
feeling? In what way or ways can it be compared with
Roots?

A. J. Seymour: There Runs a Dream p. 100

1 What has now become a dream that only the rivers
know?

2 What do you take 'History moved down river' (12) to
mean?

3 What kind of atmosphere does the poet create? How?

4 The poem is a sonnet of two parts. How do the ideas
of the two parts fit together?

List of Poems by Author

AGARD, John   *Limbo Dancer at Immigration* 43
ALBURY, Cheryl   *Poem for Mothers* 54, *Superwife* 55
ARTHUR, William S.   *The Village* 104

BARROW, Raymond   *Oh I Must Hurry* 3
BAUGH, Edward   *Elemental* 158, *This Poem* 174
BELL, Vera   *Ancestor on the Auction Block* 106
BENNET, Louise   *Colonisation in Reverse* 140, *Dutty Tough* 165
BERRY, James   *Thinking Back on Yard Time* 31
BRAND, Dionne   *Old I* 56, *Old II* 56, *St Mary's Estate* 132,
   Since You 145,
BRATHWAITE, Edward   *Adam and Batto* 129, *Discoverer* 6,
   from The Dust 22, *from Sappho Sakyi's Meditations* 162, *Hex* 115,
   His Nerves Scraped White 142, *O Dreams O Destinations* 67, *So
   Long Charlie Parker* 96, *Tizzic* 40, *Trane* 173
BROWN, Wayne   *Drought* 53, *Noah* 84, *The Black Tree* 158,
   The Visit 192

CAMPBELL, George   *Holy* 102, *The Slums* 161
CAMPBELL, Owen   *Portrayal* 175, *The Washerwomen* 11
CARBERRY, H. D.   *Epitaph* 197
CARTER, Martin   *Black Friday 1962* 170, *Death of a Comrade*
   122, *The Knife of Dawn* 197, *This Is The Dark Time, My Love*
   62, *Till I Collect* 9, *University of Hunger* 21
COLLYMORE, Frank   *Apologia* 72, *Because I have turned my
   back* 184, *Day's End* 196
CRAIG, Christine   *Crow Poem* 60, *Quadrille for Tigers* 157
CRAIG, Dennis   *Flowers* 28

DAS, Mahadai   *I Have Survived So Long* 151
DRAYTON, Geoffrey   *Still Life* 129

ESCOFFERY, Gloria   *No Man's Land* 63

FERLAND, Barbara   *Ave Maria* 30, *Le Petit Paysan* 180, *The
   Stenographer* 184
FIGUEROA, John   *Birthday Poem 1970* 174
FORDE, A. N.   *from Rain Mosaic* 123
FOSTER, Michael   *I Now Have Some Twenty Years* 181

GONZALES, Anson   *Tabiz* 93
GOODISON, Lorna   *Sister Mary and the Devil* 91
GRAY, Cecil   *Caribbean Basin* 166, *Caribbean Journal* 35

HENDRIKS, A.L.   *Albert* 13, *Like Music Suddenly* 114, *Villanelle of the Year's End* 146, *Will The Real Me Please Stand Up?* 77
HERBERT, Cecil   *Lines Written on a Train* 41, *The Sea and The Hills* 149
HIPPOLYTE, Kendel   *Choice of Corpses* 81

KEANE, E. McG.   *Country* 42, *The Age of Chains* 110

LAMMING, George W.   *Birthday Poem for Clifford Sealy* 134
LEE, Robert   *Vocation* 73

MAIS, Roger   *All Men Come To The Hills* 121, *Children Coming from School* 128
MARKHAM, E.A.   *Philpot Puzzled* 49
MATTHEWS, Marc   *Portia Faces Life* 82
McANDREW, Wordsworth A.   *Ol' Higue* 89
McDONALD, Ian   *A White Man Considers the Situation* 65, *Jaffo the Calypsonian* 69, *Yusman Ali, Charcoal Seller* 10
McFARLANE, Basil   *Afternoon Elegy* 166, *Arawak Prologue* 4
McKAY, Claude   *I Shall Return* 118, *The Castaways* 12
McNEILL, Anthony   *Ad. for a Housing Scheme* 20, *Compassionate Spider* 185, *Don* 98, *Husks* 26, *Notes on a September Day* 52, *Ode to Brother Joe* 14, *Residue* 119, *The Catherine Letter* 155
McTAIR, Roger   *Corners Without Answers* 76, *Islands* 113
MILES, Judy   *At two o'clock ...* 147, *Lunch Hour* 59, *Suicide?* 187, *Summer and Kitsilano Beach* 58
MORDECAI, Pamela   *Tell Me* 57
MORRIS, Mervyn   *Birthday Honours* 47, *Family Pictures* 46, *Judas* 189, *The Castle* 182, *The Pond* 28, *To the Unknown Non-Combatant* 64

NICHOLS, Grace   *Sacred Flame* 171

PHILIP, Dawad   *Horses* 152

QUESTEL, Victor   *Pa* 29

RAHMING, Patrick   *Mailboat to Hell* 61
RAMON-FORTUNÉ, Barnabas   *Road-Mending* 179, *The Riders* 120, *The Word Once Spoken* 189
ROACH, Eric   *Homestead* 24 *Letter to Lamming in England* 137, *March Trades* 125, *To My Mother* 33
ROYES, Heather *Theophilus Jones Walks Naked Down King Street* 79
RUDDER, David   *The Hammer* 177

SCOTT, Dennis   *A Comfort of Crows* 8, *A Family Man* 147, *Bird* 27, *Guard-ring* 94, *Squatter's Rites* 15, *Uncle Time* 96
SEALY, Karl   *The Village* 105
SEYMOUR, A.J.   *Carrion Crows* 7, *For Christopher Columbus* 108, *I Cannot Bear* 188, *There Runs a Dream* 100
SHERLOCK, P.M.   *An Old Woman* 125
SMITH, Michael   *Me Cyaan Believe It* 17
SMITH, M.G.   *from Testament* 191, *This Land* 103

TELEMAQUE, Harold   *In Our Land* 2, *Roots* 32, *To Those* 106
VAUGHAN, H.A.   *In Absence* 45, *Revelation* 35, *The Tree* 99
VIRTUE, Vivian   *Landscape Painter, Jamaica* 71

WALCOTT, Derek   *A Sea-Chantey* xix, *Adios, Carenage* 86, *After the Storm* 117, *Anna* 50, *For Harry Simmons* 72, *Homecoming, Anse La Raye* 168, *I watched the island* 167, *Mass Man* 74, *Parades, Parades* 66, *The Almond Trees* 139, *The Saddhu of Couva* 38, *The Season of Phantasmal Peace* 195
WILLIAMS, Daniel   *Letter for a friend* 193
WONG, Orlando   *I Write About* 160

YARDAN, Shana   *Earth is Brown* 36

Index of Titles

A Comfort of Crows 8
A Family Man 147
A Sea-Chantey xiv
A White Man Considers the
    Situation 65
Ad. for a Housing Scheme 20
Adam and Batto 129
Adios, Carenage 86
After the storm 117
Afternoon Elegy 166
Albert 13
All Men Come to the Hills 121
An Old Woman 125
Ancestor on the Auction Block
    106
Anna 50
Apologia 72
Arawak Prologue 4
At two o' clock 147
Ave Maria 30

Because I have turned my
    back 184
Bird 27
Birthday Honours 47
Birthday Poem 1970 174
Birthday Poem for Clifford
    Sealy 134
Black Friday 1962 170

Caribbean Basin 166
Caribbean Journal 35
Carrion Crows 7
Children Coming from School
    128
Choice of Corpses 81
Colonisation in Reverse 140
Compassionate Spider 185
Corners Without Answers 76
Country 42
Crow Poem 60

Day's End 196
Death of a Comrade 122
Discoverer 6
Don 98
Drought 53
Dutty Tough 165

Earth is Brown 36
Elemental 158
Epitaph 197

Family Pictures 46
Flowers 28
For Christopher Columbus
    108
For Harry Simmons 72

Guard-ring 94

Hex 115
His Nerves Scraped White 142
Holy 102
Homecoming, Anse La Raye
    168
Homestead 24
Horses 152
Husks 26

I Cannot Bear . . . 188
I Have Survived So Long 151
I Now Have Some Twenty
    Years 181
I Shall Return 118
I watched the island 167
I Write About 160
In Absence 45
In Our Land 2
Islands 113

Jaffo the Calypsonian 69
Judas 189

Landscape Painter, Jamaica 71
Le Petit Paysan 180
Letter for a Friend 193
Letter to Lamming in England 137
Like Music Suddenly 114
Limbo Dancer at Immigration 43
Lines Written on a Train 41
Lunch Hour 59

Mailboat to hell 61
March Trades 125
Mass Man 74
Me Cyaan Believe It 17

No Man's Land 63
Noah 84
Notes on a September Day 52

O Dreams O Destinations 67
Ode to Brother Joe 14
Oh I Must Hurry 3
Ol' Higue 89
Old I 56
Old II 56

Pa 29
Parades, Parades 66
Philpot Puzzled 49
Poem for Mothers 54
Portia Faces Life 82
Portrayal 175

Quadrille for Tigers 157

from Rain Mosaic 123
Residue 119
Revelation 35
Road-Mending 179
Roots 32

Sacred Flame 171
St Mary's Estate 132
from Sappho Sakyi's Meditations 162
Since You 145
Sister Mary and the devil 91
So Long, Charlie Parker 96
Squatter's Rites 29
Still Life 129
Suicide? 187
Summer and Kitsilano Beach 58
Superwife 55

Tabiz 93
Tell Me 57
from Testament 191
The Age of Chains 110
The Almond Trees 139
The Black Tree 158
The Castaways 12
The Castle 182
The Catherine Letter 155
from The Dust 22
The Hammer 177
The Knife of Dawn 197
The Pond 28
The Riders 120
The Saddhu of Couva 38
The Sea and the Hills 149
The Season of Phantasmal Peace 195
The Slums 161
The Stenographer 184
The Tree 99
The Village 104
The Village 105
The Visit 192
The Washerwomen 11
The Word Once Spoken 189
Theophilus Jones Walks Naked Down King Street 79
There Runs a dream 100
Thinking Back on Yard Time 31
This Is The Dark Time, My Love 62
This Land 103
This Poem 174
Till I Collect 9
Tizzic 40
To My Mother 33
To the Unknown Non-Combatant 64
To Those 106
Trane 173

Uncle Time 96
University of Hunger 21

Villanelle of the Years's End 146
Vocation 73

Will the Real Me Please Stand Up? 77

Yusman Ali, Charcoal Seller 10